Death in the Afternoon

AMERICA'S NEWSPAPER GIANTS
STRUGGLE FOR SURVIVAL

Peter Benjaminson

Andrews, McMeel & Parker

A UNIVERSAL PRESS SYNDICATE COMPANY

KANSAS CITY•NEW YORK

Library of Congress Cataloging in Publication Data

Benjaminson, Peter, 1945–
    Death in the afternoon.

    Bibliography: p.
    Includes index.
    1. American newspapers—History—20th century.
I. Title.
PN4867.B38   1984   071'.3'0904   84-14499
ISBN 0-8362-7955-7

TO
SUSAN HARRIGAN
ANNE WHITE BENJAMINSON
AND THE GHOST OF A. J. LIEBLING
AND THE MEMORY OF
JIM DEWEY
JOHN KNIGHT III
AND LADD NEUMAN

Newspapers start when their owners are poor, and take the part of the people, and so they build up a large circulation, and, as a result, advertising.

That makes them rich, and they begin, most naturally, to associate with other rich men—they play golf with one, and drink whiskey with another, and their son marries the daughter of a third.

They forget all about the people, and then their circulation dries up, then their advertising, and then their paper becomes decadent.

Joseph Medill Patterson, Founder
New York Daily News

CONTENTS

Preface

America's big-city afternoon newspapers are in trouble. Many have died.

The years 1981 and 1982 alone saw the death of five established afternoon papers—the *Cleveland Press*, the *Des Moines Tribune*, the *Minneapolis Star*, the *Philadelphia Bulletin*, and the *Washington Star*—and one newcomer to the afternoon, the *New York News' Tonight* edition.

But times haven't always been bad for America's afternoon newspapers.

They came into their own around the turn of the century as the giants of journalism—Pulitzer, Hearst, and others—thundered at each other from their afternoon platforms. The relatively primitive presses of the time could barely keep up with the demand for afternoon newspapers in America's big cities.

Since World War II, however, what many take to be a death knell has been sounding for these papers, and the ringing has become ominously loud in recent years. Most of the big-city afternoon newspapers that have not yet died have suffered serious advertising and circulation losses.

Amid such portents of doom, afternoon papers have

resorted to desperate survival tactics. Many of them, making use of the antitrust immunity given them by the Newspaper Preservation Act, have merged all but their news and editorial departments with their morning competitors.

Meanwhile, many publishers flee the afternoon, determined to fight the competition for at least a share of the morning market. They issue all-day papers, published in both morning and afternoon, usually as part of a transition from an all-afternoon to an all-morning publication.

Incongruously, while big-city afternoon newspapers are dying, merging, or becoming morning papers, their big-city morning and suburban counterparts remain healthy. The industry is strong. Daily newspaper circulation in the United States, although failing to keep pace with population growth, has reached an all-time high, and the newspaper business has become America's number one manufacturing employer, having pulled ahead of the auto and steel industries.

Changes in American society have ruined the afternoon for big-city newspapers.

Before World War II, most nonfarm employees in this country were industrial workers who went to work early in the morning and came home early in the afternoon. Though they didn't have time for a morning paper, when they got home, they wanted an afternoon newspaper to read. But service workers, who go to work later, have become much more numerous than industrial workers since the war. They have time to read the morning paper, and just as they arrive home the evening news appears on TV.

Early deadlines also hurt the big-city P.M.'s. Their staffs must write, print, and deliver the newspaper during the busiest part of the day, while news events occur all around them. By the time an afternoon paper hits the front stoop, it's already outdated. (Morning newspaper staffs have all night, when little happens, to write, print, and deliver their papers.)

When fuel, paper, and labor costs were lower, afternoon papers could put out "extra" editions reporting on news events not already covered in their regular editions. But cost increases have eliminated "extra" editions except on occasions of earthshaking importance.

Even if the afternoon papers could afford to produce "extras" every day, there would be a real problem delivering them. There are real problems delivering even the regular editions. Because newspaper readers—especially the middle-class, upwardly mobile readers favored by advertisers—have moved to outlying suburbs, just putting newspapers on their doorsteps can be a major headache. While delivery is easy enough for morning papers, which truck their editions to neighborhoods before dawn, when traffic is lightest, afternoon newspapers are delivered during the busiest hours of every day, when traffic is heaviest.

And because this country's mass-transit system has declined, there just aren't as many afternoon newspaper readers as there used to be. That most dependable of afternoon readers, the straphanger on his way home, is now preoccupied with negotiating his car through traffic jams. Further, when he does arrive home, another recent development is likely to await him—a full-scale afternoon suburban daily.

Meanwhile, the evening television news continues to attract many more viewers than morning TV news, further eliminating potential readers for big-city afternoon papers.

All these trends are exacerbated by America's advertisers, who have displayed a growing tendency to focus their advertising dollars on the top newspaper in each market. In previous eras, before radio and TV, they spread their ads among the various newspapers in each city. But rising costs have encouraged advertisers to concentrate on the newspaper with the highest—and the highest-class—circulation in each city.

As a result, whenever suburban sprawl, traffic problems, and competition from television and suburban newspapers make an afternoon newspaper the number two paper in its market, advertisers desert it for its morning competitor. This causes it to lose many more dollars than readers, leading to the incredible spectacle of papers with hundreds of thousands of subscribers disappearing overnight.

This isn't just theory.

Big-city afternoon newspapers are healthiest in the country's most industrial, blue-collar cities, such as Detroit and Buffalo, and weakest in cities where service workers dominate. They are also still healthy in some Sun Belt cities, where the general level of wealth masks the underlying reality, and in cities where geography has limited suburban sprawl.

All these trends, operating simultaneously (and, in 1981–82, in conjunction with a recession), constitute the syndrome known in the newspaper industry as "afternoon newspaper disease."

But the disease is a relatively recent phenomenon, and therein lies an additional problem.

Big-city afternoon newspapers didn't run into real trouble until the 1960s and 1970s. As a result, the owners of many of these papers began to assume they were unassailable, that they were on top and would always be on top. They ignored the oncoming deluge until it was too late. Then suddenly they were in serious trouble.

In some cities, including Washington, Philadelphia, and Oakland, the old owners sold their papers, allowing new people with new ideas to try to stem the tide. In New York City, an Australian publisher tried Fleet Street journalism, while another started a new afternoon newspaper to compete with him. And in Los Angeles, an old ownership tried revitalizing its paper there to meet the oncoming challenge.

Three of these attempts to save big-city afternoon newspapers—in Washington, Philadelphia, and New York—have failed, resulting in the death of the *New York News' Tonight* edition (1981), the *Philadelphia Bulletin* (1982), and the *Washington Star* (1981).

Three of these attempts are, at this writing, still under way, in New York (the *Post*), in Los Angeles (the *Herald Examiner*), and in Oakland (the *Tribune*).

This book is an effort to show why some of these attempts have failed, while some, so far, have succeeded.

Acknowledgments

Thanks to Jerome Aumente, Karlyn Barker, Jerry Bellune, Meg Finn, Carol Fischler, Dan Galinson, Harold Geisse, Susan Harrigan, Louis Heldman, Helen Insinger, Linda Langschied, Cheryl Spiese McKee, Richard McLain, Donna Martin, Doug Monroe, Betty Nichols, John Oppedahl, Wylbur Script, Wally Terry, and Gene Vasilew.

A note on sources. Sources are listed on pages 193–95. The listing of a source's name, however, is not meant to imply that he or she provided all the information to which his or her present or former position might be assumed to have allowed access. All opinions, errors, and judgments remain the responsibility of the author.

CHAPTER ONE

A Bigger Slice of the Brie

Giants Battle in Gotham

Dorothy Schiff didn't want the *New York Post* in the first place. Her second husband, George Backer, did. So "Dolly," an old-fashioned girl with a huge pile of old-fashioned money, bought it for him in 1939. She later dumped George, as she had dumped her first husband, and as she would dump her third and fourth husbands. But it took her a long time to dump the *Post*.

The *Post* gave her what she needed: something to do other than marry, have children, and sit on the boards of charitable organizations that wanted her mainly for her money. And the *Post* needed her. Its recurring financial crises required not only her cash but her courage, as she competed with the all-male giants of New York's newspaper arena. The *Post*'s present position as the only afternoon newspaper in America's largest city obscures its past. Then it was just one small paper, often on the brink of bankruptcy, with a gutsy but relatively inexperienced businesswoman at its helm, fighting Bill Hearst, Jack Howard, Jock Whitney, Joseph Patterson, Marshall Field, and Punch Sulzberger for survival in Gotham.

For a long while, the *Post* reflected Schiff at her best: the generous fighting liberal, the friend of Franklin Roosevelt and of Adlai Stevenson, the woman who spoke for the plain and the poor. The paper's readers, many of them Jewish and liberal, backed it to the hilt. The *Post* raged against U.S. government indifference to the holocaust. It supported strong and assertive women. It backed unionism. It stood up to Joe McCarthy. It went all out in support of the civil rights movement. Its readers went right along with it.

By the end of Schiff's reign at the paper, however, the *Post* had come to reflect her worst qualities, especially her tight-fistedness. To be sure, her parsimony was partly a reaction to the *Post*'s lean years, when the giant chain-owned dragons breathed the fiery breath of financial ruin in the face of the small and independent *Post*. It was also a reaction to rising costs and the ever-tightening squeeze on big-city afternoon newspapers.

In practice, though, Schiff's tightfistedness meant a city room with never enough desks or telephones, backed-up commodes in the restrooms, and the word "Philthy" perma-nently etched in the dust on the city-room door. More signifi-cantly, it meant little money to report on the big stories of the 1960s and 70s: Vietnam, Nixon, and Watergate. And "Dolly's" refusal to spend extra money meant reporters who spent much of their time rewriting the morning *New York Times* or the morning *New York Daily News* for the *Post*'s afternoon readers. It also meant lots of columnists.

But while the *Post* descended into blandness, enlivened only by froth, gossip, and columnists, every one of its after-noon opponents died. In 1966 Hearst's afternoon *New York Journal-American* and Scripps-Howard's *New York World Telegram & Sun*, both the products of earlier mergers, com-bined with each other and with the morning *New York Her-ald Tribune* into the impossibly hybrid *New York World*

Journal Tribune (immediately dubbed "Widget")—a morning, afternoon and Sunday conglomerate that, from the beginning, was born to lose. Squeezed by union demands and pessimistic advertisers, the new paper died only nine months after its birth, leaving Schiff's *Post* as the sole survivor in the afternoon.

Schiff had defeated all the men who had once threatened her and she had destroyed their newspapers. Here was her chance, with the competition gone, to make the *Post* a great newspaper once again, to expand its audience, perhaps appeal to the Hispanics flooding into New York or aggressively pursue the readers who had moved to the suburbs, or at least do a better job for the New Yorkers who still loyally supported the paper.

But where would the money come from?

Costs were rising steadily, and Schiff still had nightmares about her first years at the deficit-ridden *Post*. So she kept her spending down and her fears in check. Anyway, she thought, her readers had nowhere else to go. The *New York Times* was for the intellectual elite and the *New York Daily News* was for the Queens shopkeeper, and, besides, all those subway riders had to read something on the way home. After a while, though, it became evident that the lure of the morning newspaper and of the evening newscast was so strong, and the appeal of Schiff's now somewhat lightweight newspaper so weak that many people were starting to prefer nothing in the afternoon to the *New York Post*.

Afternoon newspaper disease had set in, and the paper's circulation and advertising started what looked like an irreversible decline. Between 1967 and 1976 the *Post* lost more than a hundred thousand readers. Dorothy Schiff had fought for survival before and had won resounding victories against human competition, but it began to appear that the times themselves had turned against her. By 1976, in spite of all her fiscal control, she had lost money on the *Post* for the second consecutive year. The trend was clear.

In a way, she was back to where she had started, to her first two years as owner of the *Post*, when the paper had lost a million dollars a year. But those had been exciting years. President Roosevelt had encouraged her. She had been stimulated by her new role as active businesswoman, having superseded her second husband, Backer, as the active manager of the paper. She enjoyed working with the editor and man who became her third husband, Ted Thackrey. She and Thackrey had worked together at the *Post*, struggling to make it survive as part of their marriage. Under such circumstances, the deficits, which in any case were decreasing, were emotionally supportable. But by 1976 Schiff and Thackrey had been long divorced, the deficits were increasing, and the seventy-three-year-old Schiff did not want to deal with them again, especially as it appeared that afternoon newspapers were done for.

However, the old flirtatious "Dolly" was far from dead. Her paper, with which she strongly identified, was being courted by a charming and energetic British Empire publisher, whose personal vigor and astounding publishing successes reminded her of her long-gone friend and mentor, Lord Beaverbrook.

This up-and-coming young publisher, who owned several newspapers in his native Australia, had strongly supported the Labour party there, and promised Schiff he would uphold the *Post*'s liberal traditions if she sold it to him. She also couldn't help noticing that this publisher was, like herself, an outsider. And he not only had survived, as she had, but had attracted the circulation and advertising away from his competitors, as she had.

What Schiff, so prudish about her newspaper that she once ruled that the word *abortion* would never appear in it, chose to ignore was that this publisher, Rupert Murdoch, was among the world's leading practitioners of "tits and ass" journalism. His form of journalism was not only one she would never have practiced, but one her newspaper would have had a hard time describing without violating her standards of decorum in print.

When Murdoch offered by buy Schiff's *Post*, his only other American holdings were the *National Star*, now called the *Star*, which competed with the *National Enquirer*, and the *San Antonio Express* and *Evening News*. The *News* attempted to lure that city's readers with all the sex and gore it could cram into its pages. Its readers called it the "Rape Register." Most of Murdoch's ninety-four other newspapers and magazines celebrated the seminude female body, death, the antics of well-known personalities, and little else.

Schiff, determined to sell the paper, chose Murdoch as her buyer. She had stayed just a bit too long at the party and only one boy was left to take her home. A few years earlier, she could have had her choice of numerous publishers eager to buy the only afternoon newspaper in America's largest city. S. I. Newhouse, Otis Chandler of the *Los Angeles Times*, Fritz Beebee of the *Washington Post*, and Canadian publisher Lord Thomson had all expressed an interest.

By the time Schiff decided she wanted out, however, afternoon newspaper disease was afflicting one newspaper after another, and only Murdoch was willing to brave the epidemic. He offered her $30 million for the *Post* and a way out of yet another struggle for survival. So she sold it to him.

Always the scorned outsider, Rupert Murdoch had grown to relish the role. Shy and unskilled as a youth at either sports or studies, Murdoch was scorned and abused both at his fashionable Australian prep school, Geelong Grammar, and at Oxford. In response, he struck a pose he would maintain the rest of his life: that he was excluded not because he didn't know how to do things as well as those who excluded him, but because, with his larger and more accurate vision of the world, he knew how to do things better, and was disliked because he did.

At prep school he became "Red Rupert," the radical who knew better than his fellows how the world should be organized. At Oxford he took his performance one step further by campaigning for office when doing so was strictly forbidden and was banned from a student political club as a result. From then on, Murdoch would always be the outsider, doing things others disapproved of and besting them by doing so. (One of the reasons Murdoch came to America was that he saw Americans, like Australians, as outsiders excluded from the great European centers of culture.)

That he should apply this developing behavior pattern to his newspaper ventures seemed preordained. His father was Sir Keith Murdoch, a reporter for the *Melbourne Age* who exposed the horrors Australia's troops were undergoing during the Gallipoli campaign of World War I. (In memory of this achievement of his father's, Rupert Murdoch helped produce the highly acclaimed Australian movie *Gallipoli*.)

Although Sir Keith went on to serve as chairman of Australia's Herald newspaper group, he never achieved any substantial financial interest in the chain, one of that nation's largest, and lost most of what he had to taxes at his death. (The closed circle of financiers that owned the group never permitted Sir Keith to gain more than a minor stake in it.)

This legacy of exclusion affects Rupert Murdoch to this day. He had to fight a pitched and desperate battle to retain the only newspaper left in his father's estate, the declining

Adelaide News, an afternoon newspaper his father had purchased on his own, outside the charmed circle of Herald group insiders. In doing so, the younger Murdoch had to fight the very chain that had excluded his father, and that owned the dominant paper in Adelaide.

Rupert Murdoch fought the entrenched press lords the only way he knew how: by appealing to his readers' lowest instincts. (Insofar as these instincts include lusty admiration of the female form, Sir Keith had once again shown the way for Rupert. It was Sir Keith who had staged Australia's first "beauty" contest.) While Rupert's opponents, as befitted their station, took the high road, Murdoch took the low, then stated that the resulting mass appeal of his papers—he unseated the Herald group paper from its dominant position in Adelaide—proved that taking the low road was what his opponents should have been doing all along.

It was "Red Rupert" all over again, firing his salvos from outside the closed circle of privilege, demonstrating to those within how things should be done.

The nature of his newspaper purchases underlines Murdoch's crusade to justify his outsider status, to win against the lordly insiders he sees sneering at him through the windows of their tightly bolted drawing rooms. He rarely buys into the monopoly situations other press lords sniff out— small to medium-sized one-newspaper towns in which they can squat forever, milking the community for all it will give.

Murdoch, instead, has expanded from his native Australia to two of the most highly competitive markets in the world, London and New York, where, in the glare of worldwide publicity, he can demonstrate once again that he, though excluded and despised, knows the answer to the riddle of publishing success and is brave enough to put his knowledge into action against the entrenched barons of Fleet Street and

Times Square. For a man who routinely goes up against the odds, buying a newspaper in the throes of afternoon newspaper disease, such as the *New York Post*, only added a few points against him and some extra joy to the gamble.

Shortly after buying the *Post* from Schiff (he paid 50 percent too much, he said later) Murdoch made an enemy of a former friend, *New York* magazine's founding editor, Clay Felker. Murdoch purchased *New York* magazine, *Village Voice*, and *New West* magazine out from under Felker just when the latter was trying to increase his own or his allies' stake in the company that owned all three. One of the elements that made this fight particularly bitter was that Murdoch was attempting to remove Felker from ownership of a magazine—*New York*—that Felker himself had helped create as a Sunday section in the *New York Herald Tribune*.

Felker was so devoted to the magazine, a unique mix of service features, vigorous graphics, and new-journalism-style articles, that he bought its name with his severance pay when the *Herald Tribune* itself died, then launched it as an independent magazine, and with its success, launched himself into near superstardom among journalists. (The *New York* magazine pattern, a successful attempt to appeal to young, free-spending urbanites, has been copied by city, state, and regional magazines throughout America.)

Adding to the bitterness was Felker's memory of the fate of his own father, the managing editor of the *Sporting News*, which was eerily similar to the fate of the elder Murdoch. The elder Felker had devoted thirty years to the *Sporting News* without gaining any ownership interest in the paper, and the younger Felker was determined to avoid the same fate. So when Murdoch, after winning the takeover battle, invited Felker to stay on and continue to edit *New York* as Murdoch's employee, Felker stalked out, determined to avoid the fate of both their fathers and to battle Murdoch another day. (He kept his promise later, and by doing so presented Murdoch with what appeared for a moment to be Murdoch's greatest problem, although it led to one of the Australian's greatest triumphs.)

Murdoch had beaten Felker, for the time being, but now he had to prevail over the enormous odds against him as the owner of an afternoon newspaper with a declining circulation pitted against the world's greatest newspaper, the *New York Times*, and the city's largest, the *New York Daily News*.

Within a short while, Murdoch was demonstrating how he intended to beat those odds. He shortened the *Post*'s news stories, souped up its headlines, expanded and sensationalized the paper's crime coverage, and added gossip, celebrity notes, and racetrack coverage to the small paper. Then came the Son of Sam case—and a chance for Murdoch to show the world how low the *Post* could stoop.

As the murderer who called himself Son of Sam stalked the city, the *Post*, nervous and shaking, seemed unable to control itself. "No One Is Safe from the Son of Sam!" its front page screamed, scaring the wits out of millions of readers. The day David Berkowitz was arrested for the Son of Sam murders, the *Post*'s headline screamed "Caught" in red ink.

The *Post* seemed to have tremendous pull with the district attorney, though, because its headline four days later implied that Berkowitz had been sprung from jail and had joined the *Post* reporting staff. Over the byline "By David Berkowitz," the *Post* ran the headline "How I Became a Mass Murderer." Aside from appearing to take upon itself the conviction of Berkowitz, the *Post* headline was proclaiming not a confession from the suspect, but the paper's possession of some letters he had written a girlfriend years before.

The *Post* had other causes. In the fall of 1977 the paper

endorsed mayoral candidate Edward Koch in a front-page editorial, then boldly slanted its news coverage against Koch's opponents. Fifty of the *Post*'s sixty reporters protested what they said was the *Post*'s bias toward Koch, and toward Carol Bellamy, who was running for City Council president. (Under the headline "Cinderella Carol," the *Post* ran an admiring profile of Bellamy, illustrated with photos from her family album showing her at age ten months, "with Santa at six," on her way to church, and "relaxing after a hard day's campaigning.") Murdoch's response to the reporters' written petition opposing such coverage: anyone who questioned his integrity should seek employment elsewhere. He denied any bias.

(But the walkout protesting the pro-Koch and pro-Bellamy coverage wasn't a new experience for Murdoch. According to *Esquire* magazine, Murdoch once said of Australia's Labour government, "I elected them. And incidentally, I'm not too happy with them. I may remove them." When he pulled out all the stops to do just that, using his five Australian newspapers to pummel the Labour prime minister with close encounters of the muddy kind, the staffers of one of his papers went on strike for twenty-four hours to protest their publisher's "blatant bias." Again, Murdoch denied the charge.)

In spite of its reporters' earlier protest, the *Post* so overflowed with pro-Koch fervor in 1982 that it ran coupons on its front page urging Koch to run for governor. An accompanying story encouraged its readers to sign the coupons and send them to the paper. The only catch: readers not supporting the Koch candidacy had nowhere to turn, since the coupons provided no space for negative votes. Koch took the hint and jumped into the race for the Democratic gubernatorial nomination against Lt. Gov. Mario Cuomo.

But the *Post* didn't restrict itself to politics.

Its daily offering of headlines was a potpourri of sex and violence: "Slain Woman's Mate: She Liked Me to Whip Her!" "You're Not Going to Shoot Me for a Six-Pack!" "'Death Chant' Iranians Lifted Here in Leg Irons," "Top Female Athletes May Live Together!" and that old standby, "She Kicked Her Child to Death!" When the *Post* ran a serialization of a James Bond novel and headlined one excerpt "Trapped! In Murik's Chamber of Horrors," many long-time readers of the *Post* must have felt the same way.

Something buried deep in Murdoch is revolted by all of this and occasionally pushes him in the direction of making amends. He helped produce the quality film *Gallipoli*, and his London Weekend Television produced the highly acclaimed "Upstairs, Downstairs" series. Even some of the worst of his newspapers, including the *Post*, still run thoughtful and hard-hitting investigative reports. His newspaper *Australian* remains well above the gutter level.

And in New York, what he didn't do was almost as significant as what he did do. He showed flexibility. He didn't decorate the *Post* with the total female nudity some of his overseas papers feature. (Whereas Englishmen would buy such newspapers, Americans wouldn't.) When some of the first editors and cartoonists he imported from Australia threatened to give the paper too thick a foreign accent, he changed the paper's tone.

When readers complained about other changes he had made in the *Post*, he responded. He reorganized the paper's confusing layout, put the TV section back in the middle of the sports section, and improved the paper's financial section, its sports section, and its photo reproduction. He also assigned four full-time staffers to the *Post*'s new gossip section, Page 6, which soon became immensely popular. He got rid of Schiff's less interesting columnists, added some additional conservative ones, and ran more national and metropolitan news.

The *Post* became much quicker than it had been at pursuing breaking stories. Stories that appeared in the *Post* before they appeared in the *Daily News* or the *Times* attracted and held new readers for the *Post*.

Murdoch's sensationalism monopolized public attention, though, and some press critics got off some good shots at the Australian, who was, as usual, glorying in his antiestablishment "I'll show you" pose. *New Times* called Sam "Murdoch's Favorite Son," and remarked that the *Post* made the *New York Daily News*, the former sensationalist sob sister, "look like *Our Sunday Visitor*."

News columnist Pete Hamill, who had fled the *Post*, compared Murdoch's paper to a guest who throws up at a dinner party: "He is looked on with alarm and pity, but nobody really knows what to do to help."

But no matter how he savored such establishment outrage, Murdoch saw a more substantial problem with his innovations. They didn't work, or, at least, they didn't work as well as he had hoped they would. *Post* circulation rose but *Post* advertisers fled. The people who read "nose-biter" stories, advertisers were convinced, didn't buy the high-profit, upscale goods the advertisers wanted to sell.

Murdoch, however, continued to ignore the advertisers and pursue the chimera of circulation. On two other continents, his newspapers had attracted millions of readers. He couldn't believe that he would fail to attract readers in this country; or that once he had piled up a million or two of them, advertisers wouldn't want to pursue them with ads, whoever those readers might be. (He also had a sneaking suspicion that the upscale darlings the advertisers preferred would eventually come to prefer Murdoch's journalism to that of his less sensationalist competitors.) Yet, all he seemed to be doing was replacing some of the *Post*'s liberal upscale readers with some of the city's sensation-seeking downscale readers.

Then, in early 1977, opportunity: the *Long Island Press*, its largely Queens-based circulation eroded by the New York City papers on the west and the Long Island newspaper *Newsday* on the east, finally gave up the ghost, abandoning 150,000 paying subscribers. Murdoch pounced, buying the paper's subscription list and delivering spanking new *Post*s to the bereaved *Long Island Press* subscribers for half price or less.

"The *Post* Tops 600,000 in Circulation!" the *Post* headline blared. "In one of the biggest circulation leaps in newspaper history," the *Post*'s own front-page story read in May 1977, "the *New York Post* has increased its daily sales by 122,000 in just over two months." Many of those readers slipped away, however, as soon as they had to pay full price for the *Post*— not exactly what overachiever Murdoch had in mind.

Only a year later, though, in the fall of 1978, Murdoch saw an opportunity not only to increase the *Post*'s circulation and advertising dramatically but also to play to the hilt his life-long role of the excluded and hated, yet commercially successful, entrepreneur.

In August 1978, in a recurring ritual that has dramatically raised the salaries and benefits of New York City's newspaper employees but killed off most of the city's newspapers, all the city's newspaper employee unions struck the three major papers—*Times, Daily News, Post*. This time around, though, the aggressive parties in the dispute were the three publishers. Inspired by *Washington Post* publisher Katharine Graham's successful campaign against the *Washington Post* pressmen, the New York City publishers were determined to end the overmanning in their pressrooms that was giving the suburban New York papers, largely nonunion, an economic advantage over them.

The only potential fly in the publishers' ointment was Murdoch. Shocked at the depths to which Murdoch had dragged the *Post* in pursuit of circulation, the other New York press lords could see that Murdoch was not the type to form a common front with other publishers for long. But they also, shrewdly, spotted his weakness: his desire to be a winner. So they made him president of the Publishers Association of New York City, designating him their leader and chief spokesman and champion in their fight against union greed, hoping against hope that, so designated, he'd control his desire to flout accepted standards until the striking unions were brought to terms.

For fifty-six days their scheme worked. Murdoch maintained a united front with his fellow publishers.

But *Post* history, as well as Murdoch's personality, was working against the success of the plan. During the 1963 newspaper strike, Schiff had settled separately with the unions a month before her fellow publishers had come to terms, because she feared the *Post* would not survive otherwise. She reaped an advertising and circulation bonanza as a result, but also earned the *Post* the unending mistrust of its comrades in printer's ink.

By the fifty-seventh day of the 1978 strike, Murdoch could no longer resist the same temptation. The *Times* and the *Daily News* had been making money before the strike, while the *Post* had been losing millions. It was much less able to afford a protracted strike than were its two competitors. Murdoch also had become convinced that the rich *Times*, historically liberal with its unions, would maneuver the *Post* into giving the strikers more than the *Post* could afford if the *Post* remained a party to the negotiations.

So Murdoch broke ranks, agreeing to be bound by whatever manning agreements the pressroom unions could squeeze from the *Daily News* and the *Times*. Then he settled separately with the other unions and rushed the *Post* back into publication, inheriting the Christmas advertising bonanza that would have fallen almost entirely to his two competitors. Meanwhile, the unions remained on strike against the *Times* and the *News* and kept those papers closed and profitless.

"Welcome Back" the *Post* headlines roared as the paper embraced its own return with typical modesty and New Yorkers rushed to buy the initial self-congratulatory issue and the ones that followed.

Advertisers, with nowhere else to go and with Christmas on the way, held their noses and jumped into the fetid *Post*, flooding the six-day-a-week paper with so many ads that it immediately began a 256-page Sunday edition to handle the overflow. *Post* presses hit their maximum output of one million papers per day—400,000 above the prestrike average.

As soon as the strike ended a month later, however, the advertisers and readers the *Post* had gained melted away, flowing back into their old channels like rivers after the dry season.

The return to New York normality was egged on by the managers of the *Daily News* and the *Times*, who now saw Murdoch as a traitor as well as a barbarian and set out to bleed him to death. The *News* offered its ad salesmen cash bonuses for every *Post* advertising account they could drain from the arteries of Murdoch's paper and bring back to the *News*. Every week the *News'* advertising department toted up such kills and designated the best bloodsucker "honorary pallbearer."

Within three weeks the *News'* pallbearers had something to bear—the newborn *Sunday Post*, virtually adless, died.

The *Times*, typically, took an Olympian and global view of the struggle. Rather than dirty their hands by striking out directly at their opponent, like common thugs, as did the plebeian *News*, *Times* managers decided to start a television magazine . . . in Australia. Of course, some asserted that this had nothing to do with the fact that Murdoch owned a profitable television magazine in that country and might not appreciate the competition.

With all of Murdoch's maneuvering, though, by September 1979 the *Post* had gained only 131,000 readers over Schiff's final total.

Its new total circulation of about 628,000 was smaller than the *Times'* 851,000 and was dwarfed by the *News'* 1.5 million. The *Post* didn't even have a Sunday paper to compete with the *Times'* legendary Sunday behemoth or the feisty *Sunday News*.

Even the optimistic Murdoch did not believe a marginal circulation gain such as this one could lure enough advertisers to the screaming ragamuffin the *Post* had become. As it was, Murdoch had only 7 percent of the city's newspaper advertising, against the *News'* 37 percent and the *Times'* whopping 56 percent. Meanwhile, the *Post* was losing money: $4.5 million in 1979 alone. All looked bleak for Rupert Murdoch's attempt to revive a dying afternoon newspaper by immersing it in a commode.

Despite its huge circulation lead over the *Post* and the *Times*, though, the *New York Daily News*, Murdoch's major competitor, was in trouble. Founded by Joseph Medill Patterson in 1919 as the newspaper for the common man in what was then the city of the common man, the *News* thrived until the 1970s. It had established itself during its first few years as the "picture newspaper" for the masses and had wedged its way into the public consciousness in the same way Murdoch's *Post* would capture public attention sixty years later, by titillating the working stiffs with tales of sex and violence, and with pithy bombshell headlines.

By 1923 the *News* had become the largest-selling daily newspaper in America. It hit its highest circulation ever—2.4 million—in 1947 and saw only good years ahead. But *News* management ignored the decline of the city's population and the exodus to the suburbs until the 1970s, when much of the migration already had taken place, as had the demise of all other major New York City newspapers save the *Times* and the *Post*.

(The *News* might have made an earlier effort to follow its readers to New York's eastern suburbs, on Long Island, were it not for the generosity of Col. Robert R. McCormick, the founder of the modern *Chicago Tribune*. Colonel McCormick had helped his cousin, Capt. Joseph M. Patterson, found the *New York Daily News* in 1919. As a result, the *News* is owned by the Tribune Co., of Chicago, which also owns the *Chicago Tribune* and other newspapers. But then, as uncles tend to do, Colonel McCormick got too generous and helped Patterson's daughter, Alicia Patterson, found *Newsday* on Long Island. By the time the *News* started watching its circulation fall in the 1970s, *Newsday* had been sold to the immensely rich and powerful Times Mirror Company of Los Angeles and stood in the way of any major *News* move to the east.)

The *News* tried a major move to the west by establishing a New Jersey edition in the mid-1970s, an effort similar to the *Philadelphia Bulletin*'s attempt at a separate New Jersey edition. Both efforts failed for essentially the same reason: in each area a local New Jersey paper was dominant—and advertisers were no longer interested enough in second papers to provide them with sufficient advertising. The *New York Daily News'* New Jersey section closed in 1978 after attracting a large readership but little advertising, and losing $25 million.

By the 1970s, with the *News'* circulation slipping, its managers finally realized that to get more readers and advertisers they would have to get them from New York City. They began to improve the *News*. The paper played down sex and scandal and upgraded its coverage of state and regional news with emphasis on New York City news. (The august *New York Times*, with correspondents around the world, barely seemed to notice the city at times.) The *News* also added business and entertainment news to its pages to attract the suburban commuters who worked in the city during the day and might even stick around for dinner and a show. Its subway ads featured well-known upscale types proclaiming their love for the *New York Daily News*.

Notwithstanding, the rich and the intellectual stuck with the *Times*, and the solid middle-class readers who would have been attracted by the improvements in the *News* were leaving the city in droves. The common man was fleeing New York City, leaving mostly the uncommonly poor and the uncommonly rich behind. The paper's circulation continued to drop, all the way down to 1.5 million. That it could lose 600,000 readers in just a few years—more than most newspapers ever had or expected to have—and still be the largest general-circulation newspaper in America demonstrated its immense popularity.

By the end of the 1970s, though, it had been surpassed in circulation by the *Wall Street Journal*, a paper aimed directly at the upper classes. That fact showed which way the newspaper business was going, and which way the *News* was going if it didn't do something fast.

As the *News* lost circulation it lost advertising, and thus revenue. Its costs climbed. Understandably, those facts more than normally troubled the paper's parent, the Tribune Co., which was anxious to sell its stock to the public for the first time. It had invested a great deal of money in a new printing plant for the *Chicago Tribune* and in an extensive upgrading of its Canadian newsprint operation; it needed more money for continued expansion and investment. Management hoped to garner that money through sale of company stock. But if the company's major asset, the *New York Daily News*, was on the skids financially, stockbrokers and their clients were likely to stay away rather than come running.

Mainly for that reason the Tribune Co. supported the *News* when, in 1980, that paper's management took a disastrous step. It decided to start a new afternoon newspaper in New York City. The Tribune Co. was going to gamble millions on its ability to sidestep afternoon newspaper disease in a city in which all the afternoon newspapers but one were dead, and that one, the *Post*, was losing money.

The step seemed to be, and was, sheer lunacy, but the *News* had its reasons. The main reason, as *News* executives saw it, was, what choice did they have? Their traditional readers—stable blue-collar workers, city employees, housewives—were leaving town. Advertisers were abandoning the paper as the income of the average *News* reader steadily dropped. The paper could return to the sensationalism of its past, but doing so would only signify to the world at large that the *News* was infected with Murdoch madness: the pursuit of even larger numbers of readers at greater and greater cost in lost advertisements and forsaken profits. Anyway, *News* executives could look at their own books and see that, even without imitating Murdoch, they would very shortly learn how to lose money.

The *News* needed to imitate New York's success story, not its cautionary tale, and that success story was none other than the *New York Times*.

During the first half of the 1970s, the *Times* was heading downhill with the *News*. Between 1968 and 1975, the *Times* lost 7 percent of its circulation and 21 percent of its advertising. Many people began to regard it as a paper of the past.

About halfway through the decade, however, the *Times* came up with a plan to increase its appeal to the moderately well-to-do and the highly well-to-do in New York and all over America. These people had money to spend and needed guidance in how to spend it. To keep these toffs reading the *Times* and to attract more of them, the *Times'* editors expanded the paper's sports, science, and business coverage, a step which was in many ways an extension of the paper's traditional goal of explaining everything to the experts in every field.

But the *Times* then took the additional step of adding weekly "Living" and "Home" sections to the paper. These sections covered such earthshaking subjects as what to slap on your back, what to pop into your mouth, and what to hang on your walls—fine food, tasteful clothes, and well-appointed home decor—with the same authority and thoroughness with which *Times* foreign correspondents covered the ins and outs of the Middle East peace talks.

The response to this frank appeal to upper-class consumerism, this newspaper version of Clay Felker's *New York* magazine, was overwhelmingly positive. By 1980, in spite of a still declining New York City population, the *Times* had regained the circulation it had lost during the 1960s and 70s. It also had gained back, despite the recession at the end of the 70s, more than 150 percent of the advertising it had lost. And by 1983 it actually had come within hailing distance of one million daily readers. Newspaper circulation of near a million had been reserved in this country for mass, not class, papers, but in New York City, apparently, the masses were into avocados.

This coup de Cuisinart did not go unnoticed at the *New York Daily News*. The *News*, its executives decided, would also grab for a bigger slice of the brie.

Challenging the *Times* in the morning with a *Times* imitation was out of the question. For the *News* to be remade into a legitimate challenger to the *New York Times* would cost many millions of dollars and would lose the paper the million or so daily readers who bought it partly because it was not the *New York Times*. Only one choice was left: appeal to the *Times'* audience in the afternoon, when there was no *Times*, only Murdoch's horror show.

But a great many *Post* readers were upscale suburbanites, people who read the *Times* on the morning train into Manhattan. *News* executives said that many of these people considered the *Post* an unbelievable joke, a farce, and that about 200,000 of them wanted something interesting and believable, but not sensational, to read on their way home.

Yet, if such a big audience was out there waiting for a serious afternoon paper, why had both the *Times* and the *News* specifically decided against an afternoon edition when Schiff's competitors had collapsed during the 1960s? Why, with the sole exception of the *New York Post*, had all the middle-class afternoon newspapers in New York died? But there was a substantial audience out there, *News* executives insisted, an audience for upper-class consumer journalism à la *New York* magazine—which that magazine's critics called "boutique journalism"—and for a thoughtful presentation of the news à la the *New York Times*. (*News* executives referred to these potential readers as "tie-loose" execs who wanted a "good read.")

Reasoning even more subtle was involved, however.

The *News* was losing advertising to the *Times*, primarily because the *News* readers remained relatively poor and relatively poorly educated compared to *Times* readers. If the *News* could attract upscale suburban types with its new afternoon newspaper, the average income and education level of the entire *News* readership would rise, allowing the *News* as a whole to retain its old advertisers and perhaps even attract some away from the *Times*. (*Times* executives were quite nervous about the disastrous prospect of losing any substantial proportion of their advertising to their fellow morning giant.)

To attract advertising, though, the *News'* new afternoon edition, named *Tonight*, would first have to attract upscale readers. The plan was to attack both the *Times* and the *Post*; thus, the choice of a general to lead the charge was preordained. Clay Felker was the man. *News* executives wanted him because he was the uncrowned king of upscale journalism. He would be a signal to upscale readers and advertisers that *Tonight* would be devoted to their needs and interests.

Besides, Felker already had it in for Murdoch, who had taken his beloved *New York* magazine away. In a way, Felker also had a score to settle with the *New York Times*, which had adopted his emphasis on lifestyle articles and service features as its own, at least as far as its special sections were concerned. (This identification was so strong that when the *Times* inaugurated its special sections, *Times* staffers complained they were being "Felkerized.") Considering who his two opponents would be, Felker was only too eager to climb back into the ring and have another go.

The *Times*, in public at least, took its usual magisterial wait-and-see stance toward the new paper on the block.

Murdoch, however, with very little advertising and with less than half of the *News'* circulation, could afford no such luxury, especially in the face of such a direct challenge from New York's most popular newspaper. That the new paper would be edited by Felker just added an edge to its threatening nature. Besides, after years of battling the journalistic establishment on three continents, Murdoch was not going to take such a direct threat sitting down, especially from an establishment newspaper as big as the *News.*

During the 1978 newspaper strike, Murdoch had talked about starting a new morning paper, a New York City version of his *London Sun,* a "cheeky" working-class scandal sheet featuring bare-breasted "crumpets." He had come to realize that what worked in London, where the working class liked to shock the establishment, wouldn't sell in New York, where the working class liked to think of itself as middle class, and was. He never began his *New York Sun.* Now Murdoch saw an opening. The *News* was not only challenging the *Post* in the evening, but leaving itself vulnerable in the morning. Murdoch made an historic decision. He would start a morning edition of the *Post* to compete with the morning *News* and *Times.* His new morning paper would be stylistically identical to his afternoon paper.

With these two decisions, the *New York Daily News* and the *New York Post* began long runs up separate blind alleys. The *News* was going after the high-spending readers that advertisers wanted, but by launching an afternoon newspaper in New York City, it was sailing a bark into the Bermuda Triangle in pursuit of them. On the other hand, the *Post* was going from the time slot of the dying to one that would allow it to attract readers and advertising. But in doing so, it had to compete head to head with a newspaper that had more than twice its circulation and more than five times its share of the city's newspaper advertising. Nevertheless, each paper selected its chosen field of battle. Murdoch, always in character, struck first, launching his morning *Post* in July 1980. The *News* followed with its *Tonight* in August.

Thinking big, as always, the *News* hired several hundred new employees to put out the new paper. *Tonight* had something for everyone. To the upscales it offered what amounted to an afternoon *New York Times* (without the extensive intellectual, worldwide news coverage that paper is famous for), plus a new *New York* magazine. It featured six new sections—"Manhattan," "1st Person," "At Home," "Style," "Getting Ahead," and "Sports Extra"—which resembled similarly named sections in the *Times*. These also appeared in the morning *News*. It also offered the upscales long trendy features, think pieces, columns, analyses, expanded business and financial coverage, and the late stock-market report.

To the blue collars it offered merely an update of the morning *News* plus the late race results. Much of *Tonight* was similar to the morning *News* and appeared even more similar than *News* executives would have liked. Because of production problems, both the morning *News* and the *Tonight* edition had to be tabloids.

But *Tonight* editors set their hearts on attracting the morning readers of the *Times* (not the morning readers of the *News*) on their way home. Ads for the new paper urged New Yorkers to read not only *Tonight* at night, which might have been expected, but the *Times* (not the *News*) in the morning. The editors of the morning *News*, incensed that their own offshoot would urge their readers to switch to the competition, complained to Mike O'Neill, *News* executive editor, about the ads. O'Neill replied that the ads were not meant as a reflection on the *News'* morning readers.

Tonight was a high-quality newspaper aimed upscale, but its tabloid size and other problems made it appear to be aimed at both upscales and downscales. *News* management was making the same mistakes it had made when it tried to appeal to both upscale and downscale readers by making the morning *News* more serious and important. In many instances, what repelled one sort of reader attracted the other and diluted the newspaper's essential character.

Tonight's upscale offerings, though, were so well put together that its blurred identity wouldn't have been fatal had it been a morning newspaper. But by offering serious, well-crafted journalism, *Tonight* ran into a major additional problem that afternoon newspapers like the the *Post* don't have to face. People start the day full of hope and dreams and expectations. They will do something important that day, make something of themselves. Many are eager to read a paper that will prepare them for the productive day they're sure lies ahead: a paper like the *New York Times* or the *New York Daily News*. Anyway, they've been asleep for eight hours and want to know what's happening in the world.

At night, after a long dreary day of disappointments and revelations of their own inadequacies, they want something that will take their minds off reality and transport them to an exciting fantasy world.

Perhaps, if they're able to envision themselves as the sadistic criminals featured in the *New York Post*, it's a world in which easy vengeance is available.

If they see themselves as among the day's victims, they want to know that whatever has happened to them that day is not as bad as what happened to the other guy. And of that the *Post* generously and graphically informs them. You're still alive, it tells them. You haven't been "Strangled by a Sex Attacker." Your house and family are fine. They haven't been

"Hurt in an Acid Rampage" or "Pummeled by a Furious Pimp" or "Clubbed to Death." So why not stop worrying?

In this sense, the *New York Post* is the "good-news" newspaper that community and religious groups all over America have been demanding for years. After all, is good news how well your competitors are doing or how well you're doing in comparison?

Even those who don't see themselves as criminals or as victims, and don't wish to see harm befall their neighbors or their competitors, can find something in the *Post*. With its personalized approach to news coverage, the *Post* had become a sort of daily news-oriented *People* magazine that talked in a folksy way about what people were doing all over the world. What's new with the marines in Lebanon? What's new with our troops in Grenada? Read the *Post* and find out.

The *Post* reader, after flushing hotly, or cluck-clucking, at the latest sex scandal, could easily adjust to the warmth the rest of the paper provided, the intimacy of a global village in which each reader could share in the triumphs and losses of his fellows and in which all could think and feel as one.

Before it tried climbing upscale, the *News* was the virtuoso of this sort of journalism. Captain Patterson personally conducted his reporters and editors on tours of New York City so that they could keep in touch with the people's concerns and the people's speech and not drift off into middle-class dreams as they sat at their desks in the News Building.

But the *News*, during the *Tonight* period, seemed to be deaf to the sensitivity it once had with the vox populi. When a former all-Ireland accordion player was found shot to death in his car in Queens, a friend of his told the *News*: "I'd like to get hold of the mutt that murdered him. I'd be judge, jury, and executioner. He was the sweetest man you'd ever want to meet and he never hurt a soul." Here was a chance for a newspaper that wanted to immerse its readers in the warmth of fellow feeling to run the story on its front page with the headline "I'll Get That Mutt!" But the *News*, dreaming its own dreams, buried the story on page 5, and awarded it the weakest possible headline: "Accordion Champ Slain."

On another occasion, in August 1980, a truck carrying explosive propane gas sprang a leak on the George Washington Bridge. The driver pulled off onto an exit ramp into Manhattan and halted the truck. Officials, fearing an explosion, closed the exit and the bridge, causing a traffic jam that stretched for thirty miles and lasted seven hours. Hundreds of thousands of people sat trapped in their cars listening to news bulletins or just wondering what was happening. Unsuccessful attempts were made to stop the leak. Finally, two New York City emergency service cops, both former plumbers, got fed up. They bought a $4 plumber's plug, walked over to the truck, and hammered the plug into the leak. They took a big chance but solved the traffic problem: the truck resumed its journey, releasing what seemed like the entire world from terminal grid lock.

The *Times* ran a story about the incident on its front page, accompanied by two photographs, one of the truck and one, from a distance, of the backed-up traffic. It also ran several additional stories about the incident in its second section. The *News* also covered the story thoroughly.

The *Post*, however, ran a photo the full width of the front page showing the two cops triumphant atop the truck. Above the photo, in headline type reserved by more respectable papers for the end of the world, the *Post* ran the word "Thanks!" For the hundreds of thousands in their cars who had been involuntary participants in this drama, this was monumentally successful journalism. The *Post* had expressed their feelings and had become one with them.

When Murdoch first bought the *Post*, the editors of the *News* closeted themselves with copies of Murdoch's other publications, looking for ways to fight him. Rather than giving up and trying to imitate the *Times*, they might have tried imitating the seductive warmth and sexual crackle of his journalistic style.

Tonight ran into a more prosaic problem as well, one that has bedeviled afternoon newspapers all over America: traffic. The *News'* circulation department, unaccustomed to afternoon traffic conditions in Fun City, had a painful time getting *Tonight* to the newsstands on time during the rush hour. As a result, the paper's primary targets had trouble getting it. When the paper's editors tried for an earlier deadline, in order to deliver the paper to the stands on time, they found that they couldn't always publish the final stock-market report in the paper, thus drastically reducing *Tonight's* attractiveness in the eyes of exactly those upscale readers it had hoped to attract.

All these problems manifested themselves as one gigantic problem: *Tonight* didn't sell. Aimed at a potential audience of 210,000, *Tonight* never exceeded 120,000, and dipped to 80,000 during the summer. Although this figure was disappointing, the underlying reality was tragic: *Tonight* had replaced the *News'* former "Night Owl" edition, which, operating with a skeleton staff, had sold 80,000. So the *News'* millions of dollars and hundreds of new employees seemed to be bringing it, at most, only 40,000 new readers (out of a 1.4 million total). This was at *Tonight's* peak, when it was still the object of lively curiosity among New York's newspaper readers. The novelty soon wore off, though, and *Tonight* skidded downhill.

Deeply concerned, *News* executives offered up an $800,000 ad campaign to tout the new paper. Nothing happened. Frantic with worry, they trimmed the number of pages in the paper and shortened its stories, both to cut costs and to attract new readers with brevity rather than bulk. Still nothing. Felker moved from editor to consultant, and was replaced by an old-line editor interested more in straight news reporting than in the price of artichokes. Still nothing.

Meanwhile, Murdoch, spending much less to print an early edition of the *Post* than the *News* was spending on *Tonight*, seemed to have fallen into a honey pot. *Post* circulation started to climb steadily, reaching 934,000 by 1982, with more than half of it in the morning.

Murdoch had neatly sidestepped death in the afternoon. He also had done something else perhaps even more extraordinary. He had expanded New York City's newspaper-reading audience while the city's population continued to decline.

Without additional advertising, though, each extra *Post* Murdoch printed added to his losses. In 1981 he admitted to losing $10 million annually on the paper, but vowed to go on indefinitely and "bleed the *News* to death within five years." But it was Murdoch who was doing the bleeding. In 1982 the *Post* lost $20 million.

Tonight, though, was doing worse than nothing. While the *News* struggled to keep *Tonight* aloft, the *New York Times* gained readers and ads and the *Post* gained readers. Even the morning *News* gained readers, while *Tonight* seemed suspended in space, slowly losing altitude, a target for the gibes of the opposition.

Near the end, *Tonight*'s editors realized that New York's afternoon newspaper readers would buy only the *Post* or its equivalent. So they added a red streak to *Tonight*'s nameplate, more titillating headlines to its front page, and more sensationalism to its stories, but once again *Tonight*'s circulation barely budged.

Finally, one year and millions of dollars after founding *Tonight*, with its circulation at 70,000, the *News* closed it for good, laying off 320 of its new employees.

News executives, disgusted with the afternoon, didn't even bother to revive the old "Night Owl," the afternoon edition *Tonight* had replaced, although the "Night Owl" had sold 127,000 copies as recently as 1977.

The *News'* audacious and amazing attempt to start a new afternoon newspaper in Gotham had failed. Now it would pay the penalty.

CHAPTER TWO

Death Moves
to the Morning

The *News* Takes a Stand

For a short time after *Tonight*'s collapse, *New York Daily News* officials merely said they were disappointed that *Tonight* hadn't produced the revenues they needed to offset the losses they saw in the *News'* immediate future.

To minimize these losses, they announced a series of layoffs, salary freezes for nonunion employees, and elimination of some bonuses and fringes. Even with these measures, they said, the paper would lose $12 million in 1981 and $50 million in 1982. *News* executives began conferring with the paper's unions about the situation and preparing to ask those unions for financial and other concessions.

Meanwhile, the paper attempted to reattract more of its traditional blue-collar readers with shorter, newsier stories, zingier headlines, larger photos, more features, and fewer analyses.

News editors also announced they would concentrate on the five New York City boroughs and nearby suburbs and forget about the outlying and outstate areas—which they had clearly lost to their suburban competitors.

Readers started coming back to the *News*, and its circulation edged up slightly. As it did so, the *News'* editors claimed to be optimistic.

The paper, however, by inspiring Murdoch to start a morning edition, had lost its major advantage: its morning mass-
market monopoly. Were there enough blue-collar and
middle-class readers in New York City and environs to keep
the *News* going, now that those readers could choose the
Post, as well as the *News* or the *Times*, in the morning?

The *News* had other problems as well. Its losses were
likely to keep increasing unless the Tribune Co. spent money
to make the paper more efficient. Particularly needed was
$60 million to renovate the *News'* Brooklyn printing plant
and to consolidate its printing there. That was not an unrea-
sonable expenditure, considering the sixty years of profits
the Tribune Co. had made on the paper, and the possibility of
future profits, especially if Murdoch got tired of losing
money and closed the *Post*.

The Tribune Co., however, had other plans for its accumulated profits: it already had decided to spend $33 million to
buy a major cable TV system and $20.5 million to buy the
Chicago Cubs baseball team to have something to show on
that system. It also had closed its afternoon newspaper in
Chicago, *Chicago Today*.

It was, in short, losing interest in the newspaper business,
and to continue to finance its expansion out of that business,
the company had become more intent than ever on going
public. A leaky flagship such as the *News* might prevent it
from doing so with maximum profit, but if the company
dumped its nonprofitmaking assets, it could go public profitably. Anyway, now that the company was into TV and
baseball, what did a newspaper matter? *Tonight*'s failure
certainly hadn't added to the *News'* allure at the Tribune Co.

Therefore, when Robert Hunt, *News* publisher, proposed
the Brooklyn printing plant renovation, Tribune Co. bosses
asked Hunt if he could guarantee them sufficient profits

from his new investment. When he said he couldn't guarantee such profits, they threw up their hands and told Hunt,
only four months after *Tonight* closed, that they would
spend no further money on the *News* and that they were
putting it up for sale.

James Patterson, a Tribune Co. stockholder and the son of
News founder Joseph Medill Patterson, called the decision to
sell the *News* "a tragic error."

It is "particularly ironic," he said, "that our company's
management is willing to dispose of the *News* as one would
throw out yesterday's newspaper."

With the *News* now squeezed between the *New York
Times* and the suburban papers on one side and the *New York
Post* and television on the other, many wondered who would
buy it. It was widely believed that chances were good that no
one would, and that the Tribune Co. would then close the
paper. *News* sports columnist Dick Young saw such bleak
prospects ahead that he jumped to the *Post,* which, in cele-
bration, filled half its back page with a photo of the columnist and his family. Indeed, the Tribune Co. was taking quite
a chance that the *News'* advertisers would follow Young's
lead. Announcing that a major newspaper is for sale has long
been considered its death knell and an everyone-overboard
warning bell for advertisers.

As if to punctuate the alarm everyone felt about the *News,*
three bandits held up its Brooklyn printing plant, the very
one Hunt had requested $60 million to renovate, and blithely
robbed it of $125,000 in cash.

The truly worried parties, though, were the *News'* own
employees, who began arranging for an employee attempt at
purchasing the paper if no viable commercial purchasers
showed up.

Union adviser Theodore Kheel asked New York government agencies to provide the *News* with tax credits or low-interest loans. Although the request was understandable from Kheel's point of view, it's hard to see how government subsidy of the *News* would have been consistent with freedom of the press.

Such subsidies would have been consistent with newspaper owners' attitudes, though. If the government threatens to tax newspapers or control their news content, then the publishers accuse the government of interfering with the sacred freedom of the press guaranteed to American journalists by the Founding Fathers. If the government allows newspapers to join together in combinations that would otherwise violate the antitrust laws, or gives them money, however, then the government is only doing its duty by America's largest manufacturing industry.

Although a number of media outlets have accepted government money or tax credits, including ABC, *Newsday*, and *Reader's Digest*, the Tribune Co. rejected any such aid on the grounds that accepting such assistance might interfere with the sale of the paper, since the new owner would want to be the one to negotiate the terms on which such aid would be given.

The *News* would have had problems attracting buyers even without Murdoch or its own need for renovations. It was carrying extra weight aplenty. When it was the only popular morning newspaper in town it had continually yielded to union salary and staffing demands. As a result, *News* employees were paid for duplicating each other's work, for playing cards, or for just staying home.

Meanwhile, at the *Post*, Schiff had held down spending as much as she could, and Murdoch had not only inherited the benefits of her thrift, but laid off a large number of *Post* employees when he took over the paper. Thus he ran a relatively lean operation in comparison to the bloated *News*.

But hope springs eternal in the hearts of those with enough money to buy a newspaper as big as the *News*.

On first hearing that the paper was for sale, real estate people all over America salivated at the thought of what they would do with the *News'* spectacular Manhattan skyscraper on Forty-second Street and Second Avenue, the model for the Daily Planet building and the spiritual home of the big-city newspaper worshiper in us all. Then the Tribune Co. announced that the building itself was not for sale.

To the surprise of many, a number of other businessmen who wanted to keep the *News* going as a newspaper also expressed an interest. It was, after all, America's largest general-circulation newspaper, was published in the morning, and had been losing money for only a few months.

Among those expressing an interest were Warner Communications, which seemed to have holdings in every area of communications except newspapers and saw a place for the *News* in its lineup; John S. Dyson, chairman of the New York State Power Authority and former publisher of a group of weeklies; Arthur Levitt, Jr., American Stock Exchange chairman; real estate developer and businessman Donald Trump; real estate developer and *Atlantic Monthly* magazine publisher Mortimer Zuckerman; and Loews Corporation magnates Laurence and Robert Tisch.

Murdoch couldn't help twitting the *News* and ran a story in the *Post* suggesting that Rev. Sun Myung Moon was interested in buying the paper. The *News'* managers furiously denied the story. That's all they needed, for their readers to get the impression that the *News* was a Moonie organ. There were many worse candidates around, though. At least Moon had lots of money. A company he founded was already backing a New York City newspaper, the *News-World* (later the *Tribune*). His Washington, D.C., newspaper, the *Washington*

Times, was respectable and Moon seemed willing to absorb its losses forever. He probably would have been willing to underwrite the *New York Daily News'* losses, too, just for the immense prestige of having respectable newspapers under his aegis in the two most important cities in the U.S.

There were even stranger aspects to the sale of the *News* than the possible participation of the South Korean evangelist.

The sale, in fact, was not a sale in the usual sense, in which buyers offer money to sellers for items the sellers want to part with. The Tribune Co. was offering the *News* itself, its printing plants, its fleet of trucks, a newspaper distributing company, newsprint at a discount for five years, a half-price lease on the *News'* offices in the News Building, and $45 million in presale severance payment costs—a $100 million package—to anyone who would agree to assume the obligations of running the paper. Greatest among these obligations were the millions of dollars that would have to be paid its employees in severance and other payments were the *News* to be shut down after it was sold. The "sales negotiations" involved the buyers demanding more and more from the *News* for assuming these risks—or shying away when the risks, coupled with the *News'* long-term problems, became apparent to them.

Soon, all were eliminated except Trump and one other: the man who had done it all before, the man who had bought and sold the *Washington Star*, banker and newspaper publisher Joe Allbritton. Now was Allbritton's chance to outmaneuver the competition again, save a great newspaper—a paper that towered like a monolith over every paper he then owned or ever had owned—and walk away with his Texas-sized pockets jingling.

First, Trump had to be eliminated. Very soon, he was.

Trump wanted the *News*, but refused to assume any of the liabilities of shutting it down until 1987, although Trump and the Tribune Co. would split the paper's operating losses and ownership until then and Trump would arrange financing for a new printing plant for the paper. Trump's offer also was conditioned on his success in reaching agreement with the *News'* unions on cutting costs at the paper. It was a mark of the Tribune Co.'s pecuniary desperation that Trump's offer was so seriously considered that a detailed letter of intent was prepared based on it.

At the last moment, however, the Tribune Co. told Trump he had to assume responsibility for the closing costs as soon as he reached an agreement with the unions, rather than five years later. This ruptured the tentative agreement between the Tribune Co. and Trump and left the door open for Allbritton. He told the Tribune Co. that if he could wring certain salary and job-cutback concessions from the *News'* unions within thirty days, he would assume immediately thereafter the obligations of running, and, if necessary, of closing, the *News*.

Not a man to fool around, and a man, moreover, who was used to having his way with unions, Allbritton stunned the New York unionists on his first meeting with them. The unions had envisioned a potential total loss of about 500 jobs, but Allbritton demanded the elimination of 1,800 jobs (out of 5,000 at the *News*), $80 million a year in givebacks, a wage freeze, and a contract guaranteeing no strikes for five years. He also reportedly wanted permission from the unions to hand-pick the employees to be laid off—mostly older employees—rather than follow union seniority rules in choosing his victims.

It was easy for Allbritton to propose such draconian measures, since the Tribune Co. had promised to pay the severance and pension costs of any employee Allbritton could cut from the *News* payroll before taking over the paper, up to a total of $45 million.

Except for wanting the unions to pay the company, prohibiting them from making wage demands, prohibiting them from striking, emasculating their seniority system, and laying off over a third of their members, Allbritton wanted nothing from the unions at all. (Allbritton did offer the unions something, though: 20 percent of future *News* profits and a series of wage increases after the wage freeze ended.)

He also prevailed upon the *News* to help him shove his demands down the union members' throats by declaring him to be the "buyer of last resort." The *News* was announcing, in other words, that unless the unions agreed to Allbritton's demands, the Tribune Co. would shut down the *News* for good. Like a nutcracker, the Tribune Co. and Allbritton squeezed the unions between them.

The unions, refusing to be squeezed, said they considered the "last resort" statement an "unacceptable ultimatum."

Allbritton was assuming that if the unions yielded, he'd be able to run a profitable *Daily News*. He also was hoping that if the unions made concessions to him, the other newspapers in town wouldn't demand a piece of the action and force the *News'* unions to retract the concessions they had made. (The other papers were entitled to identical concessions under their contracts with the unions.)

Of course, if the owners of the *Times* and the *Post* waived their rights to a few extra dollars, Allbritton could successfully buy the *News* and it would not be shut down, the only alternative envisioned at the time.

Murdoch refused to waive his rights. He already was losing millions on the *Post* and needed all the givebacks he could get. What he didn't need was revived competition from the *News* under the resourceful Allbritton.

The *Times*, however, was making millions. And, in the words of a *Times* executive, "The more newspapers there are, giving different points of view, the better off a city is and the better off a people are." *Times* executives actually had complained in print that if the *News* went out of business, it would cause problems for the *Times*. Many former *News* readers would start buying the *Times*, but *News* readers were not as attractive to advertisers as *Times* readers were. Therefore, *Times* executives argued, inheriting the *News'* readers might actually lose ads for the *Times*.

Whatever the merits of this argument, the *Times* just couldn't let go of the money it would lose by not demanding of its unions the same concessions that Allbritton was demanding of the *News'* unions. *Times* stockholders, the paper's executives said, could not be convinced that the company needed to give away millions of dollars it could have demanded for its own coffers just to keep a competing paper, with a larger circulation, in business under a new and aggressive management.

In their insistence on identical concessions from their unions, *Times* executives made it clear that their high-minded paper, always far above the petty circulation wars that swirled at its feet, would not spend any money of its own or of its stockholders to keep a competing newspaper, its only half-serious competitor, alive in America's media center. No matter how much prattle about the responsibilities of giant corporations its editorial writers might turn out, the *Times* knew where to draw the line.

Both the *Times* and the *Post* were prepared to act purely in their own interests if the *News* folded. *Times* and *Post* ad salesmen were poised to swoop down on the *News'* advertisers. Murdoch had gone so far as to rent enough printing capacity to turn out two million *Posts* a day so that he'd be able to pick off the *News'* readers before nearby suburban vultures, such as the always lurking *Newsday*, could make a determined assault on them.

The union leaders weren't foolish enough to hope that Allbritton was engaging in a mere bargaining ploy; they knew his record as a tough negotiator at the *Washington Star* and at his New Jersey papers too well.

In desperation, seeing years of layoffs, cutbacks, and salary freezes before them under Allbritton, or possible lifetime unemployment if his bid failed, they asked Murdoch to make an offer for the *News*. The union leaders pointed out that concessions to the *News* might jeopardize the future of the *Post*, and where would that get them? They were interested in jobs, not competing theories of journalism. Murdoch, they said, might have the best chance of saving both papers.

Murdoch, who has never in his life failed to respond to a challenge, asked the Tribune Co. for the right to bid for the *News*.

Not only were the unions asking him to bid, he had heard that the Tribune Co. was giving the *News* away, rather than selling it, and he couldn't resist taking a long shot at bagging his major competitor, the nation's largest single-market daily newspaper, for nothing.

Murdoch insisted that his proposal was the soul of logic, since, in his words, the *News* and the *Post*, under separate ownerships, were "engaged in a dance of death which must end in the disappearance of one or both newspapers." He proposed that he and the unions buy the *News* as partners and then spend $150 million to build a new printing plant capable of printing both papers. He pledged to maintain both the *Post* and the *News* "as separate and independent newspapers, serving their different audiences and faithful to their individual traditions and history."

Murdoch, however, was already putting out a morning and an afternoon paper. What did he need with another morning newspaper in the same city? It was ads he needed, not readers. If he bought the *News* and killed it, he might lose readers who couldn't stomach the thought of switching to the *Post*, but he would gain almost all the *News'* advertisers, who needed a mass-market New York City newspaper to sell their wares.

Anyway, both Murdoch and the Tribune Co. knew that the historic end to a newspaper war is the purchase of the losing newspaper by the winner. The winner then proceeds to absorb some of the loser's readers and advertisers, sometimes even to print the loser's name in small type under the large name of the winner on the winner's masthead, and to shut down the losing paper itself for good. Murdoch certainly could have run a very efficient operation had he been able merely to double the circulation of the *Post* and fill the comparatively adless *Post* with the *News'* ads, without having to hire the *News'* staff.

There were real questions, in any case, about whether the U.S. Justice Department would have allowed Murdoch to operate two of the three general-circulation daily newspapers in the nation's largest city. (He might have been allowed to run both papers under a joint operating agreement, but such an agreement would have required that control of the *News'* editorial content remain in hands other than Murdoch's, and it was editorial content that Murdoch saw as the road to eventual profit.) Stanley Cook, Tribune Co. president, charged Murdoch with a "transparent attempt to destroy and shut down the *Daily News*," and refused even to meet with the perpetual outsider.

The *News'* employees, still not exactly thrilled about the looming prospect of being thrown out on the street, with little likelihood of getting a job elsewhere, continued their efforts to be heard. If none of the other bidders was successful, they, the employees, would buy the *News*. Members of all ten of the production unions at the *News* went so far as to vote to put a pay raise they received into a fund to underwrite the purchase of the paper.

Like small children in a roomful of sumo wrestlers, however, they had a hard time getting the Tribune Co. to take them seriously. Both the Tribune Co. and the union leaders themselves saw a major problem with a union purchase of the *News*: money. What if the unions bought the *News*, but then couldn't prevent it from going under and throwing all its employees onto the street? How would it look if the unions weren't able to pay their own members the severance pay and benefits due them? Both sides saw a union purchase only as a last-ditch move in case all else failed.

But no matter how frightened the unions were, or how unenthusiastic about owning their own big-city newspaper, they just couldn't swallow Allbritton's terms. His demand for no wage increases for five years was particularly distasteful to them. The unions also were worried that Allbritton might force them into major concessions and then sell the paper for a big-buck profit. And they just didn't believe the Tribune Co. would fold a paper that had lost only 3 percent of its gross revenue in 1981, including the losses on the *Tonight* edition, considering the immense closing costs involved.

As the unions became more balky, Allbritton asked for five extra days to reach a settlement with them. During that period, the unions rejected his demands and came up with a counteroffer of their own. Realizing that his initial approach to the unions was not going to be the overwhelming blitz he had hoped for, Allbritton became pessimistic. Both he and the Tribune Co. concluded that, with his momentum gone, Allbritton wasn't going to be able to bring the unions around and his attempt to purchase the *News* would not succeed. The Tribune Co. called off his bid.

Allbritton had come close, though. He certainly had shocked the unions. The Tribune Co. also had been shocked. It wasn't until its highest executives started talking seriously about closing the *News* that they realized how much it would cost to padlock the Daily Planet. Like a giant version of its weekly nemesis, the Sunday *New York Times*, the *News* was hard to get rid of without paying special hauling charges to have it dragged away. When the doors at Forty-second Street and Second Avenue slammed shut, the Tribune Co.'s checkbook would drop open with an even more resounding thud. The first check would be a whopper: $90 million in pension and severance payments to *News* employees. And that, Tribune Co. executives had come to realize, might be only the beginning. The Chicagoans had guaranteed lifetime employment to the *News'* printers, and employment through March 1984 to the paper's pressmen. Breaking that guarantee while there was still a chance of selling the *News* might result in a suit for $100–$300 million in damages, as soon as those doors clanged shut.

To make matters worse, the Tribune Co.'s lawyers said they couldn't guarantee that the company could successfully defend itself against such a suit. This bomb was dropped on the Tribune Co. execs along with the realization of how much the *News'* union members had seriously considered sacrificing to keep the *News*, and their own jobs, alive.

Suddenly, the company sniffed a whiff of what it needed to stay in the newspaper business—profit. If the unions had come so close to disemboweling themselves for Allbritton, they'd probably be willing to shoot themselves in the foot a few times if it would help the Tribune Co. start making money once again on the *News'* readers and advertisers.

Once more the Tribune Co. waffled. Originally it was going to save the *News* with *Tonight*. Then it was going to sell the *News* to Allbritton, or close it. Now it suddenly decided that, no, Allbritton was not the "buyer of last resort," and that rather than give the *News* away, the Tribune Co. would keep it.

Groping tearfully in the dark, the unions and company found each other and hugged each other tight.

Thankful that it wouldn't be losing its $300 million just yet, the Tribune Co. immediately pledged to invest $90 million in the *News* to keep it operating and return it to profitability. The company pledged to spend $44 million of this amount building satellite printing plants for the *News* outside Manhattan. (The company subsequently financed all this by selling two thirds of the *News'* most valuable asset, its headquarters building, for $90 million, retaining only that portion of the building the *News* itself used.)

This time around, Tribune Co. execs made their investment contingent on major concessions from the unions: the elimination of 1,340 jobs, 460 fewer than Allbritton had wanted, but still over one quarter of the total *News* payroll. They eased this blow by refusing to ask for a wage freeze, or wage givebacks or cuts, and by offering bonuses of $30,000 to $120,000 each to union members who retired early.

Although such buyouts would cost the Tribune Co. $48 million, once the former staffers had been paid off they would no longer have to be paid regularly and the *News* would save millions each year in salaries. (Because both Murdoch and the *Times* were still standing greedily by, the Tribune Co. managed to arrange the concessions it demanded so that the two other papers wouldn't be able to demand similar concessions under the "me-too" clauses of their union contracts.) The company then backed these proposals with a threat to close down the *News* by 1984 or earlier if the unions didn't come through.

A threat to close down the *News* before the aborted attempt to sell it would have been greeted with hysterical laughter. After watching the Tribune Co. come so close to selling the *News* to Allbritton, however, the unions were in no mood to call the company's bluff. Eventually, one by one, they voted to give it what it wanted.

Joe Allbritton, by playing the bogeyman, had saved another newspaper, but he couldn't have done it alone. Union demands for high wages, featherbedding, and lifetime job guarantees had finally come full circle: after helping to kill off most of New York City's newspapers, they had helped save its largest, perhaps for good.

In what could be taken as a tribute to Allbritton, the final agreement between the Tribune Co. and the unions contained an Allbrittonesque touch: *News* employees were promised 24 percent of the paper's profits above 6 percent, a first for a unionized newspaper. The supercapitalistic Tribune Co. had brought semisocialism to the New York City newspaper industry.

With its immediate fate finally settled, the *News* went back to doing just what it had been doing before the Tribune Co. decided to head upscale with the *Tonight* edition: trying to reattract the solid working- and middle-class readers that once kept it in luxury. More crime, sex, celebrity, and entertainment news, more and larger photos, and bigger and blacker headlines were added to the paper, to help it struggle against the *Post*. It added consumer news and money-management features as well to help it compete with the *Times*.

The paper used its new printing plants, outside Manhattan, to print eight separate editions of the *News*, every day except Saturday, for each of the five boroughs of New York City, and one for each of three close-in suburban areas.

The suburban sections, rather than attempting thorough coverage of the suburban areas in competition with the local papers, aimed principally at conveying New York City news, as well as lifestyle, arts, business, and entertainment features, to those suburbanites still close enough to New York City to feel its attraction and be interested in its doings.

It remains to be seen how successful these sections, and the *News'* other attempts to regain its former readers, will be. *News* circulation began to increase again, then dropped once more in late 1983. *News* executives blamed the new losses on the turmoil surrounding the construction of the new plants. And some of the readers the *News* was attracting were the same sort of readers Murdoch was attracting: people who wanted to play the *News'* Zingo, Instant Zingo, and Super Zingo games as opposed to or in addition to the *Post's* Wingo game. (Both are bingolike games that flaunt large cash prizes. They are aimed at attracting new readers and advertisers, but advertisers are unimpressed by such games because the players don't keep buying the paper after each contest ends. So, the theory goes, the games cost the papers more in the long run than they're worth bothering with, although they do serve to increase circulation as long as they appear in the paper.)

The great Wingo vs. Zingo competition gave each paper and owner a chance to show its latest stuff. Murdoch was able to demonstrate his love for big gambles: he started the *Post's* Wingo game by mailing out six million free game cards to surprised Mr. and Mrs. Occupants. He then upped the weekly Wingo jackpot to $100,000.

These gestures, and related contest costs, were estimated

to have cost the *Post* $3 million in 1981 alone, a sizable percentage of the paper's overall loss that year.

Murdoch also used Wingo to demonstrate his continued ability to attract readers without attracting advertisers: industry analysts estimated Wingo gained the *Post* 100,000 new subscribers but little if any new advertising. He also was able to display his penchant for sob stories and his ability to pluck the heartstrings of the great global village with news flashes about Wingo winners, headlined with such gems as "Wingo Suits Maria to the Grand!" about a thousand-dollar winner.

The *News* demonstrated its ability to imitate the *Post* in other ways. Without either spending the vast sums the *Post* was willing to spend or showing the same flash the *Post* showed, it was attracting as many useless and expensive new readers as the *Post*. The *News* didn't mail out any free cards, promoted its Zingo games less lavishly, and gained 100,000 new readers. Its Zingo headlines, however, showed no particular genius for anything but straight reporting. "Widow and Son Win $50,000 Super Zingo" was one gut-grabber.

News management also demonstrated its newfound ability to put its foot in its mouth. In an interview with the *New York Times*, James Weighart, *News* editor, was quoted as saying that the *News'* own game, Zingo, "stinks." This, of course, gave Murdoch the opportunity to prove once again that he was not a gentleman among gentlemen. For the next week, ads in the *Post* screamed: "The Editor of the *Daily News* admits it: 'Zingo Stinks' . . . and he should know!" Weighart dusted off the oldest excuse in the burned source's lexicon and said he was "quoted out of context."

More significantly, the *News* started making money again only a few months after wringing concessions from its unions.

Death in the Afternoon

48

After losing $11 million 1981 and $14 million in 1982, the paper made $6 million in the first half of 1983. Largely responsible was the $48 million the paper claimed to be saving annually on labor costs as a result of the union concessions, but its advertising, aided by New York City's recovery from recession, was on the way up as well.

Unfortunately for the *News*, though, advertisers did not return to the paper's "Sunday Magazine." Because ads must be submitted to the magazine much earlier than to the other sections of the paper, the "Sunday Magazine" advertisers pulled out as soon as they heard the *News* was for sale, recognizing this announcement as the traditional prelude to closure. Even after the Tribune Co. announced that the *News* would stay open, few advertisers returned to the magazine.

Finally, *News* publisher Hunt added *Parade* magazine to the *Sunday News* to supplement what had become a totally anemic home-grown product. *Parade* joyously welcomed four million new readers with two-page ads, which quoted Hunt describing *Parade* as "part of our commitment to bring *Daily News* readers a stronger, better-looking, and more interesting newspaper."

He might as easily have said, The company almost killed our magazine with its indecisiveness, forcing us to pay good money for a syndicated product just to make our Sunday paper look like a Sunday paper.

If the *News* ends up killing its own "Sunday Magazine" and relying on *Parade* as its Sunday supplement, New York's demanding readers will have to be content with the same magazine fare available in 133 other American newspapers.

With the Tribune Co. scared back into the New York City newspaper business, at least in part by the high costs of getting out of it, the *News'* immediate future looks secure, although the paper is still stuck with the seemingly intractable long-range problems that almost brought it to grief in the first place: the *Times* is taking the high road and the *Post* is taking the low road, and the middle road in New York City, where the *News* is trapped, is constantly narrowing. Within a few years, the paper may hit the center-lane divider and disintegrate in flames.

Still, the *News* has fulfilled its immediate destiny as far as the Tribune Co. is concerned; with the paper back in the black, the company was able to go public successfully in late 1983, garnering all the cash it needed to continue its expansion into televised entertainment or elsewhere.

Meanwhile, Murdoch, inspired by the *News'* example, and bolstered by the *Post's* growing readership, decided to make a run at profitability. The first step was easy. He raised the price of the *Post* from twenty-five cents to thirty, a move that seemed to have little if any effect on the paper's circulation while reducing the *Post's* losses from $20 million to $11 million a year. (The *News* raised its price to thirty cents a few months later.)

Next Murdoch moved against the same unions that had given the *News* so much and asked them for similar concessions, which would have allowed him further to reduce his annual losses on the *Post*, from $11 million to $9 million. The unions were aware, however, that Murdoch was floating in cash, and that a man of his determination, especially with his money, was unlikely to close a paper in a city as prestigious as New York just because he was losing a few million on it. So the unions refused. If you were working in the *Post's* composing room, would you want to sacrifice your next raise to help a multimillionaire international press lord reduce the losses on one of his many newspapers from $11 million to $9 million? The unions told Murdoch he could continue to finance the *Post* out of his own pocket.

Indeed, Murdoch's worldwide magazine and newspaper publishing empire doubled its profits in 1983. His raunchy British newspapers, the *News of the World* and the *Sun*, were highly profitable, and losses were cut sharply at his *Times* of London and *Sunday Times*. His newspapers in San Antonio, Texas, as well as the *Village Voice* and *New York* magazine, both in New York City, and the nationally distributed *Star*, were all spewing out profits, and the *Boston Herald* was beginning to produce them.

His businesses were so flush with financial health that in 1983 he paid $97 million to buy the *Chicago Sun-Times*, putting him in competition with yet another Tribune Co. paper, the *Chicago Tribune* itself. He also spent $98 million that year buying stock in Warner Communications, aiming at eventual control of the firm, as if to punish it for even thinking of buying the *New York Daily News* and thus entering the lists against him.

(Two could play this game. *Chicago Sun-Times* publisher James Hoge, who hoped to own the *Sun-Times* but was outbid by Murdoch, signed on with the rival Tribune Co. and was immediately sent to New York as the *News'* new publisher to compete with Murdoch in that city.)

Besides, Murdoch was getting more than empty prestige from the *Post*; he was piling up political clout. Because of his willingness to slant the *Post*'s news and editorial columns in the direction of the candidates he favored, Murdoch had earned the slavish gratitude of New York City's politicians. He tried to add to this political pull by having the *Post* sponsor speeches and forums at which political incumbents and candidates appeared before audiences of civic leaders and other influential persons.

Murdoch may have been using some of this pull to extract benefits for his other businesses. Shortly after he had lunch with President Carter at the White House in 1980 and told Carter the *Post* would endorse him for renomination, the U.S. Export-Import Bank, a federal agency, approved an unusually low-interest loan of $206 million. The loan went to Murdoch's Ansett Airlines, one of Australia's two domestic airlines and Murdoch's biggest nonmedia holding, to help that company purchase twenty-one Boeing jetliners. The loan was granted without a formal application from Murdoch.

Both Murdoch and the Carter appointee who administered the bank denied any connection between the promise of endorsement and the approval of the loan, and a U.S. Senate inquiry found no evidence of impropriety. Yet the timing raised the question of whether Murdoch's losses on the *Post* were real or superficial.

The war of nerves between the *News* and the *Post* continued. Who would be the first to break? The international press lord, or the midwestern conglomerate? The atmosphere grew acrimonious. *News* editor Weighart called the *Post* a "jokebook" and "hyped-up crap" and said Murdoch's only choices were to "go on losing money" or "become a real newspaper." But two of Weighart's executives cracked under the strain. They were arrested for attempting to pay a $20 bribe for an advance copy of the *Post*'s Wingo game card. As part of Murdoch's response, the *Post* dubbed Weighart "Potato Head."

Pressure was added to the conflict as many *News* and *Post* readers continued to move to the suburbs, and the suburban papers, not happy gorging themselves on former New Yorkers, began to move slowly into the city itself. *Newsday* added staffers to its city edition, increased the percentage of Manhattan news in it, and announced it would open a Manhattan news office.

Murdoch's losses continued, with the *Post* still laying claim to only about 8 percent of New York City's total newspaper advertising. As the city's second-ranked popular newspaper, the *Post* continued to have difficulty attracting ads, although *Post* executives asserted that their paper's readers were as upscale as the *News'* readers, and that their paper would eventually get the amount of advertising its large and growing circulation deserved.

Would it? New York's big advertisers were of the same social class as, and in some cases were the personal friends of, the toney executives at the *Times* and the *News*. They said they didn't like Murdoch's newspaper, and they may not have. Few advertisers want their products associated with rapes and murders, if they have any choice. But what really annoyed them was Murdoch's style. They didn't like the way he seemed to be trying to buy his way into the upper levels of New York's politics and society, as indicated in part by the *Post*-sponsored forums. Along with their fellow major employers, the publishers of the *Times* and the *News*, New York's big advertisers had been shocked when Murdoch broke with his peers and started publishing on his own during the 1978 strike. Besides, they said, we're already appealing to the downscale audience through the *News* and through television and to the upscales with the *Times*. So why advertise in the *Post*?

Murdoch also remained a victim of afternoon newspaper disease. His circulation growth was occurring in the morning while his afternoon circulation had shrunk to 240,000, less than half of the *Post*'s afternoon circulation in its last days under Schiff. Yet Murdoch had to continue putting out an afternoon *Post* each day, at tremendous expense, or lose his identity.

Murdoch the gambler may have lost his chance to supplant

the *News* with the *Post* when the Tribune Co. and its unions finally decided to support their paper for the indefinite future. Unless Murdoch is willing to continue to bankroll the *Post*'s losses indefinitely, his paper may collapse under the weight of those losses long before the *News* is squeezed out of New York along with the city's remaining middle class.

Meanwhile, through attempting to save a declining afternoon newspaper, Murdoch had made his mark on the Big Apple—by indirectly reinvigorating an old morning paper, the *News*, and starting a new one, the morning *Post*.

CHAPTER THREE

Big Oil to the Rescue

The *Philadelphia Bulletin*

In 1949 Walter Annenberg, publisher of the morning *Philadelphia Inquirer* and the afternoon *Philadelphia Daily News*, proposed that his newspapers join in partnership with the majestic afternoon *Philadelphia Bulletin*, the voice of the city's aristocracy and the paper that proudly advertised, "In Philadelphia, nearly everybody reads the *Bulletin*." Annenberg proposed that the two companies put out a morning, afternoon, and evening paper jointly. "It would have been like shooting fish in a barrel," Annenberg said later. "It would have meant $5 to $10 million a year in profits for each of us." He suggested the two companies split the profits of the proposed partnership fifty-fifty.

But the *Bulletin* publisher, Maj. Robert McLean, demanded 60 percent, because the *Bulletin* and the McLeans were dominant and prestigious. Indignantly rejecting the demand, Annenberg told a *Bulletin* executive, "Someday the major is going to learn . . . that pigs go to the slaughterhouse." Many years later Annenberg was to remark that the owners of the *Bulletin* were nice people, but they "had a certain arrogance they were unaware of."

By 1969 Annenberg, then American ambassador to Great

Britain as well as Philadelphia's media czar, was worried. For weeks, speeding in his big black limousine from one London cocktail party to another, rain spattering on the car's bulletproof windshield, Annenberg worried not only about Anglo-American relations and American business interests, but about his broadcast-newspaper empire, Triangle Publications, Inc., in Philadelphia. To be sure, all his properties, including the *Inquirer* and the *Daily News*, *TV Guide*, *Seventeen* magazine, WFIL-AM and -FM radio, and WFIL-TV, were making money. And of course there was no one to stop the ambassador from continuing to use the *Inquirer* and the *Daily News* for his own purposes.

Walter Annenberg was a man of great angers, and when he was angry with someone, that person's name did not appear in any publication Annenberg owned, no matter what fame that person achieved. Among those who had dropped from sight after clashing with Annenberg were singer Dinah Shore, University of Pennsylvania president Gaylord P. Hartwell, and former ambassador to Ireland Matthew McCloskey.

Annenberg didn't play around when someone was on his blacklist. Once, when he had to print a picture that included McCloskey, he airbrushed McCloskey out. When he had to cover the campaign of Milton Shapp, whose candidacy for governor of Pennsylvania in 1966 he strongly opposed, he beset him with unfair and vindictive stories.

But Annenberg couldn't see that he had much need for the *Inquirer* anymore. After all, his good friend Richard Nixon had appointed him ambassador to the Court of St. James. And although his first few months as ambassador had been embarrassing—he had spoken "awkwardly" to Queen Elizabeth on their first meeting and had become embroiled in several controversies—Annenberg was a determined man and he was determined to make a success of his London assignment.

Once he did, his national and international prestige would be ensured. He would no longer need the *Inquirer* and the *Daily News* to buttress himself against the social scorn he had endured ever since his father—publisher, businessman, and race-wire king Moses Annenberg—had been sentenced to three years in the federal penitentiary for income-tax evasion. Annenberg couldn't even look forward to passing the paper on to his son. (That son, Roger, who had been ill for years, had committed suicide in 1962.) Most worrisome of all, there might soon be governmental opposition to Annenberg's continuation as Philadelphia media czar.

Shapp, who hadn't appreciated running an uphill race for governor in the teeth of virulent abuse from Annenberg-owned media, had attempted to turn the government against Annenberg. One hundred fifty years ago, after the abuse he had taken from Annenberg's newspapers during the campaign, Shapp might have challenged Annenberg to a duel, or assaulted the ambassador with a cane on the public street. But the video era had arrived, and Shapp decided to strike back at Annenberg in a less personal and potentially more damaging way.

Shapp filed a petition with the Federal Communications Commission charging Annenberg with "censoring, omitting, twisting, and distorting" news, and "using it for personal vengeance." Specifically, Shapp's petition opposed Annenberg's right to continue to run WFIL-TV, Annenberg's Philadelphia TV station.

The TV station was one of Annenberg's most profitable holdings. He didn't want to give it up just yet, but the ambassador was a realist. He knew the FCC frowned on businessmen who owned newspapers and television stations in the same city, believing such arrangements gave one person too much control over the area's news. And Triangle included not one newspaper and one TV station in Philadelphia, but two newspapers, two radio stations, and a TV station there. Years later, Annenberg said that Shapp's petition influenced him not one iota. But the ambassador was well aware that no one else in America owned such a' concentration of media holdings in a single market. He also saw, correctly, enormous publishing potential in *TV Guide*, now America's most popular weekly magazine, and less potential in his Philadelphia newspapers. So Annenberg decided to avoid a potentially distracting and damaging confrontation with the FCC by, in his words, "telling on it before it told on me." He decided to end his near domination of the Philadelphia media.

In October 1969 Ambassador Annenberg sold the *Philadelphia Inquirer* and the *Philadelphia Daily News* to Knight Newspapers, Inc. for $55 million.

Although few realized it at the time, Annenberg's signature on the sales contract might as well have been a signature on the death warrant for the proud *Philadelphia Bulletin*. The executives of what was once America's largest afternoon newspaper (both the *Washington Star* and the *Los Angeles Herald Examiner* also held this title for a time) had no idea what was about to hit them, even though they should have.

Knight already had demonstrated, in Miami, Detroit, Charlotte, and elsewhere, that it could build newspapers into formidable competitors through fierce, determined, expensive, and high-quality journalism, coupled with a little hard dealing when necessary.

After a couple of years of preparation, the *Inquirer*, under executive editor Gene Roberts, began winning Pulitzer Prizes and didn't stop. During the mid-1970s it won six consecutive Pulitzers in five years, a record that caused one local wag to suggest that the *Bulletin* attract reader attention by beginning a campaign against Pulitzer Prizes in general.

The *Inquirer*'s investigative teams exposed U.S. foreign aid (for bypassing the poor and going to the rich, discouraging agriculture in underdeveloped countries, supporting sweatshops abroad, and throwing Americans out of work), the Federal Housing Administration (for allowing speculators to make killings on urban renewal), Philadelphia's criminal courts (for victimizing the poor), the international oil crisis (revealed as phony, since the same amount of oil reached the U.S. during the "crisis" as before), the IRS (for discrimination against middle-class taxpayers) and the Philadelphia police (for routinely beating suspects).

The *Inquirer* sent one of its reporters through medical school, and for four years his stories, "The Making of a Doctor," were widely noted. The paper opened foreign bureaus, investigated the bloated and corrupt state legislature, and covered the suburbs with sweep and panache. Its editorials called in clear and simple language for change and reform.

Meanwhile, the *Philadelphia Daily News*, the afternoon newspaper Knight also had purchased from Annenberg, provided the sort of solid, only mildly sordid tabloid-style coverage that appealed to blue-collar readers.

As the *Inquirer*'s circulation began to catch up with the *Bulletin*'s, the *Bulletin* fought a losing battle on several fronts. Whereas *Inquirer* editors had an uncanny knack for choosing stories carefully, giving them extensive first-rate coverage, and making them informative and interesting, the *Bulletin* covered everything, and everything it covered seemed dull.

The *Inquirer*, taking full advantage of Knight's corporate resources (in the mid-1970s Knight swallowed the Ridder

Newspapers to become Knight-Ridder, Inc.), sent its own highly skilled reporters to world trouble spots, from which they sent back fascinating and informative stories aimed at Philadelphia readers.

Meanwhile, the *Bulletin* devoted a sizable portion of its resources to covering local school board meetings and neighborhood controversies, trying without much flair to compete against Philadelphia's forty-nine suburban papers and one hundred weekly papers in exactly those reporting situations those papers handled best. The *Bulletin* even tried to go head to head with the suburban papers by publishing separate daily suburban editions, an effort that greatly drained its corporate energies and coffers. Nineteen reporters and editors were assigned to the *Bulletin*'s New Jersey edition alone, trying to cover every city council and school board meeting in that state.

The *Inquirer* countered by increasing its coverage of Trenton, New Jersey's capital, and by sending reporters out into the suburbs only when something spectacular happened. Meanwhile, the two *Bulletin* reporters assigned to Washington, D.C., tried frantically to compete with the *Inquirer* and Knight-Ridder's battery of nineteen reporters stationed there. When Three-Mile Island almost melted down, the *Inquirer* flooded the site with reporters, while the *Bulletin* responded with only a few staffers and second-rate coverage.

The *Bulletin*'s style of coverage made a lot of sense when most Philadelphians were blue-collar workers who lived within the city limits. These readers wanted to know, in detail and with great accuracy, what was going on in each of their neighborhoods.

But during the 1960s and 70s, many of Philadelphia's residents moved to its suburbs, where the area's suburban papers provided them with all the local coverage they needed.

Increasingly, their suburban neighbors, and many city residents, were white-collar workers whose interest had been widened by education and by transfers all over the country and, in some cases, all over the world. *Inquirer* editors realized that these new readers looked to their metropolitan papers for a window on the world, not a suburban or inner-city bulletin board. *Inquirer* management also realized that such readers were very attractive to advertisers.

The *Bulletin*, however, like the *Washington Star*, tried in large part to be a local Associated Press for its readers, providing them with the sort of coverage that already had lulled generations to sleep in their overstuffed easy chairs, eyes slowly closing behind their bifocals.

The *Bulletin*'s managers argued that the coverage the *Bulletin* was providing—mostly straight, local news reporting, not particularly national or international and not particularly investigative or analytical—was exactly the coverage *Bulletin* readers wanted. The paper's circulation figures argued otherwise.

In retrospect, it's also hard to see why the paper's managers thought the best way to compete against the suburban papers was to maintain the *Bulletin* as a pale imitation of its suburban rivals.

Bulletin readers who wanted to know the whys and wherefores of a news event were helped little by the paper's editorial page.

During one of Richardson Dilworth's campaigns for mayor of Philadelphia, the story goes, an aide rushed up to him and breathlessly thrust a *Bulletin* editorial under the candidate's nose. "The *Bulletin* has endorsed you!" the aide shouted. Dilworth read the editorial. "How can you tell?" he asked. He might have been talking about all the other *Bulletin* editorials as well.

The standing joke at the paper was that whenever a *Bulletin* editorial writer found that he'd boxed himself into a corner and had to venture an opinion on a subject, he'd suggest at the end of the editorial that the subject be approached "with less heat and more light" and stop writing, leaving his readers staring at the cliché in disbelief. One editorial writer was overheard assuring his boss that while he planned to write an editorial on a controversial topic, "We don't have to touch the controversial part."

In an attempt to help the *Bulletin* compete more effectively with the *Inquirer*, both Robert L. Taylor and William McLean III, grandson of the paper's founder, who succeeded Taylor as publisher in 1975, cut some of the spot news out of the paper, added some analysis, and brightened the *Bulletin*'s makeup.

Then, in 1978, McLean launched a morning edition of the *Bulletin* to compete directly with the *Inquirer*. If he had tried this a few years before, when the Knight Co. was just getting the *Inquirer* organized, and the *Bulletin* was the dominant newspaper in town, McLean might have forced Knight out of the city. But by 1978 it was too late.

Bulletin executives, though, had reason for some optimism when they launched their morning edition. At last it looked as if they had an ally in their unequal contest with the high-flying *Inquirer* and the industrious *Daily News*.

That ally was just about the unlikeliest person the Philadelphia Main Liners who ran the *Bulletin* could have imagined: Pierre Peladeau, one of North America's great hustlers. Peladeau also was known as Pulpy Pierre, a reference to his tacky publishing empire, and Pierre Pile-o'-Dough, a reference to his not so tacky publishing revenues. Peladeau had founded his empire in the 1950s by purchasing a failing bilingual weekly near Montreal for the gigantic sum of

$1,500. By appealing to mass tastes, Peladeau had increased his holdings to twenty-two Canadian newspapers, twenty-two magazines (sold in Canada and the U.S.), eight printing plants, and an ink-making concern.

So equipped, Peladeau marched on Philadelphia.

For years, bleeding-heart scholars of the media have lamented how prohibitively costly it would be to start a newspaper anywhere in America these days—to say nothing of how much it would cost to start one in America's fourth-largest city, in competition with a dominant locally owned institution such as the *Bulletin* and two strong chain-owned products like the *Inquirer* and the *Daily News*. Peladeau didn't have too many buddies in academe, though, so he had no one around to tell him that you can't do what he did: start a new daily newspaper in Philadelphia, the *Journal*, for only $1 million, half of which he borrowed. Upper-class Californians were buying only moderately impressive single-family homes for the same amount at about the same time.

One of Peladeau's secrets was avoiding investments in real estate or in heavy equipment. He rented a vacant supermarket across the street from the *Bulletin*, bought fifty used typewriters, fifty used desks, and fifty experienced news people, and, one Friday in 1977, put them all together with instructions to get the first issue out by Monday.

They did, and from day one the paper they produced looked like a winner. It covered crime, sports, and sex to the exclusion of almost everything else. It also featured in each issue a "Philly Filly," a local girl displaying some portion of her body for the reader's edification.

The *Journal*'s first issue sold 200,000 copies, and even a few weeks later, after the novelty had worn off, the paper was averaging 150,000 sales a day. Peladeau asserted that by selling the paper for twenty-five cents a copy, ten cents higher than his competitors' price, he could make a profit on sales of only 80,000 papers a day. He was exaggerating, but his competitors began to worry.

The truly challenged party in this journalistic *mélange à quatre* was Knight-Ridder's *Daily News*, the afternoon tabloid that banked on appealing to the same blue-collar audience Peladeau was gobbling up. *Daily News* management was worried enough to add seven reporters to its eighty-five-member staff and expand the paper's coverage.

The *Inquirer*, although not directly challenged by the pulpy new tabloid, added more racing results, more sports news, and a gossip column to its pages, but otherwise remained committed to the journalistic high road, which, according to circulation and advertising figures, seemed certain to lead it to the top spot in Philadelphia's newspaper competition.

(Not that the *Inquirer* stuck slavishly to the high road in its competition with the *Bulletin*. In 1977 the *Inquirer* saw the chance to strip the poor old *Bulletin* of one of its most popular features, Doonesbury, and secured exclusive Philadelphia-area rights to that feature. The *Bulletin*'s executives, gentlemen all, were shocked that anyone would stoop to such a trick, but thousands of their readers weren't too shocked to switch over to the *Inquirer* in pursuit of the comic strip.)

Bulletin execs breathed more easily as soon as they saw what Peladeau was doing. Many of the readers they might have lost to the new *Journal* had been lost to the *Daily News* some time before.

As far as the *Bulletin* was concerned, Peladeau brought some justice to the Philadelphia newspaper wars. While Pulpy Pierre bombarded the *Daily News* with sports scores and cheesecake, the *Bulletin* would be left free to bounce the

Inquirer around a bit. Besides, the *Bulletin* was making money on the *Journal*. The canny Canadian wasn't going to tie up money in a composing room and printing presses when the *Bulletin* was right across the street. In fact, he paid the *Bulletin* to print the *Journal*.

For the *Bulletin*, the *Journal* was a dream come true: it increased the *Bulletin*'s revenues, threatened its competitors, and left most of its readers alone. Peladeau was noncompetitive with the *Bulletin* in another way as well: he ran no editorials at all.

Nevertheless, displaying all the symptoms of afternoon newspaper disease, the *Bulletin* kept declining in circulation and watched its advertisers depart.

Bulletin publisher McLean decided in 1980 the jig was up. Playing the role Walter Annenberg had played thirty-one years previously, McLean proposed to his fierce foes over at the *Inquirer* and *Daily News* that the two companies enter into a joint operating agreement. Such an arrangement would allow the two companies to keep their news and editorial operations separate, but combine their circulation, advertising, and other departments, thus saving millions in duplicated expenses. JOAs are exempted from the antitrust laws under the federal Newspaper Preservation Act of 1970, if one of the newspapers can be proved to be failing.

Knight-Ridder agreed. The company had spent five difficult and expensive years rebuilding the *Inquirer*, and even after the five prize-winning years that followed, was still not certain that the *Inquirer* was the wave of Philadelphia's future.

Then, tragically, McLean pulled out of the negotiations. He had no illusions that he could turn the *Bulletin* around on his own, but he didn't want to underwrite the *Bulletin*'s losses for the one to two years it would take the government to approve the proposed JOA. He decided that his only hope was throwing in the towel.

Who would buy the battered *Bulletin*?

Almost everyone in the news business knew that the paper was struggling not only against two determined and well-financed opponents, and its owners' misjudgments, but against the dread afternoon newspaper disease as well. What the despairing McLean needed was someone with a lot of money who had reason to be optimistic about the news biz, afternoon division.

Suddenly, as if in answer to a prayer, Warren Buffett inquired about purchasing the *Bulletin*. Buffett certainly had a lot of money. He also was one of those renaissance entrepreneurs who seem to do well in all sorts of businesses, being the controlling shareholder of Blue Chip stamps, a major stockholder in and board member of the *Washington Post*, and the owner of Sees Candy.

The owner of a dying afternoon newspaper might well turn to Buffett for succor in any case, since another of Buffett's major holdings was the *Buffalo Evening News*, an afternoon newspaper that was doing so well it would drive Buffalo's morning newspaper out of business two years later. But Buffett's interest went no further than an inquiry.

The next pigeon to walk toward the *Bulletin* trap was even richer, and much more impetuous: Raymond Mason, high-rolling president of Charter Company, a petroleum conglomerate.

Mason was a perfect buyer for the *Bulletin* because he had already gambled and won. In part by buying a half interest in a Bahamian oil refinery just before oil prices rose dramatically in the late 1970s, Mason had increased Charter Co.'s profits from $23 million in 1979 to $365 million in 1980, a 1,468 percent increase still talked about on Wall Street. Anyway, owning minerals and newspapers is an old and honored tradition in American publishing. William Randolph Hearst supported his entry into New York City journalism with the money from the sale of his mother's copper mines. (The tradition continued: Arco Oil owned the *London Observer* from 1976 to 1981.)

Mason loved buying magazines and newspapers. With the spare change left over from his success with the Bahamian refinery and other ventures, he had bought into the company that owned *Family Weekly*, *Ladies Home Journal*, and *Sport* magazine. With his remaining mad money, he picked up *Redbook* and, in a move some later saw as a dramatic foreshadowing of his experience to come in Philadelphia, bought Billie Jean King's faltering *WomenSports* magazine and let it die. He wouldn't have been Raymond Mason if he hadn't made money doing all this. His 1979 publishing profits were $800,000. On revenues of $175 million, however, this came close to losing money, and Mason realized he'd need some help in choosing his future purchases.

It was about this time he met Karl Eller, a man who had done with publications what Mason had done with his oil-related purchases: turned them into gold. Starting out in billboards, Eller had built an empire that included thirteen TV and radio stations, the *Cincinnati Enquirer*, and the *Oakland Tribune*.

In 1979 he sold this entire collection, now called Combined Communications, to Gannett Newspapers, the nation's most prosperous newspaper chain, for $370 million worth of Gannett stock, making him Gannett's largest shareholder and giving him a seat on that company's board of directors. (That Eller had made his fortune partly by investing in a big-city afternoon newspaper, the *Oakland Tribune*, blinded him to one of the *Bulletin*'s flaws and made him a perfect partner for Mason in purchasing it.)

Eller stayed with Gannett only a short while. A restless entrepreneur, he resigned after clashes with Gannett's management—"There wasn't room for two chief executives at Gannett," he said later—and vowed to build another media empire. But Eller needed capital. And Mason needed someone who had done well with media properties. The two men got together and formed Charter Media Company. Its ambitious goal: $100 million in annual profits within five years. Buying media properties capable of producing such profits would be expensive, however; most newspapers and television stations carried big price tags.

Then Eller's eye fell on the ailing *Bulletin*. Although its circulation was falling and its advertising dropping away, the *Bulletin* was still a well-known and prestigious publication. Besides, publisher McLean, desperate to leave his sinking ship before most of his advertisers beat him down the gangplank, was hawking the *Bulletin*, its physical facilities alone worth $10–$15 million, for an embarrassingly paltry $2 million in cash and the assumption of $29 million in promissory notes. "He was giving it away," one expert noted. On April 30, 1980, Charter Media bought the *Bulletin*.

While the purchase was being negotiated, an attempt was under way to reach a JOA pact like the one almost arrived at between McLean and Knight-Ridder. The two companies arrived at an informal arrangement that would have made Philadelphia a rarity in journalism by preserving all three of the newspapers involved—the *Inquirer*, the *Bulletin*, and the *Daily News*—in a joint operating agreement. (Surveys indicated there was so little overlap between the *News* and the *Bulletin*, although both were published in the afternoon, that Knight-Ridder-Charter would have been gaining a larger audience and more advertisers by publishing both the *Bulletin* and the *Daily News* in the afternoon as well as the *Inquirer* in the morning.)

Only the Sunday *Bulletin* would have ceased publication as a result of the arrangement. But the *Bulletin*'s owners hadn't even bothered to start publishing a Sunday newspaper until 1947, so the Sunday *Bulletin* had only 50 percent of the Sunday *Inquirer*'s circulation and 20 percent of its advertising share. (If the Sunday edition had been begun years earlier, it would have kept the *Bulletin* going years longer.) And publishing only one newspaper on Sunday would have avoided the necessity of combining the very different *Bulletin* and *Inquirer* into what would have been one overwhelmingly schizophrenic Sunday product.

Sunday aside, such a JOA, which would have preserved and revitalized two afternoon newspapers and one morning paper in the same city, would have been strong medicine against afternoon newspaper disease (although *Bulletin* executives insist that for various other reasons the JOA wouldn't have been that great for the *Bulletin*). The entire edifice, however, soon came crashing down around the heads of its proponents. Some say the reason was . . . a reception held the night before the final JOA negotiating session.

It was the sort of reception a town's leaders would throw for anyone who had put his or her own money behind one of the town's faltering major businesses. At this particular reception, arranged in honor of the *Bulletin*'s new owners, Karl Eller was feted and lionized by Philadelphia civic leaders, who told him how strongly they supported him in this fight of fights. What an historic personage he was for attempting to save the *Bulletin*, they told him. How important it was that the *Bulletin* maintain its historic independence! Most of what they said was the sort of thing that would be said at any similar reception, but Eller, who was in any case among the most competitive of entrepreneurs, took the praise and pledges of support to heart, according to some sources. Eller withdrew from the proposed agreement. He would fight it out alone.

Eller said later that, in retrospect, he should have gone ahead with the JOA. But, in Eller's version, what prevented him from doing so wasn't all the praise and adulation, but the section of the proposed joint operating agreement that would have required him to spend large amounts of money on marketing and promotion to maintain the *Bulletin*'s still large circulation during the year or two it would have taken government agencies to approve the JOA. Knight-Ridder insisted that Eller underwrite the *Bulletin*'s circulation in this way so that Knight-Ridder would be guaranteed that the *Bulletin* it would eventually own jointly with Eller and Charter would be worth owning.

Once Eller decided against a JOA, all the white flags were put away for the duration. A ferocious eleventh-hour struggle to save the *Bulletin* began.

To help lead the *Bulletin* forces, Eller hired as the *Bulletin*'s new publisher N. S. (Buddy) Hayden, another man who had made a lot of money buying and selling newspapers. Hayden had started at the *Miami Herald* as a copy boy in 1958, and four years later, with a friend, had purchased a Georgia weekly for $80,000. In four more years, he had sold that paper for triple his investment and had become the publisher of a series of newspapers in larger and larger cities, finally hitting the big time in Philadelphia.

Also hired, to run the *Bulletin* under Hayden, was Craig Ammerman, who had been serving as *New York Post* managing editor.

Hayden and Ammerman tried energetically to make up for much of the time the *Bulletin*'s original owners had lost, but the *Bulletin* was in the same predicament in which a marginal neighborhood business might have been in 1929. No matter what was done, very little was likely to save it.

There was only one thing to do, though: make sure all the colorfully wrapped goods were out front, to attract the customers the paper so desperately needed.

First, as befitted a paper in its death throes, 120 nonunion employees were laid off or convinced to take early retirement, and wages were frozen. That none of these employees was from the news or advertising staff showed management's commitment to the paper's survival, management said.

Cutbacks and wage freezes were only a beginning, however. Within a short time, the *Bulletin*'s new owners changed it from a somewhat stolid paper to a boldly colorful, very horizontal paper full of eye-catching charts and bar graphs. These charts and bar graphs came to be extremely elaborate and informative.

One graphic—accompanying a *Bulletin* story on nearby Atlantic City's casinos—displayed, for each casino, its revenues for that month, the changes in its revenues compared with those of the preceding month, the average daily win at that casino that month, its yearly gross to date, its years since opening, its taxes paid to date, and its taxes paid since opening.

A front-page story in the Sunday *Bulletin* about plans to reduce local rail service provided by the South East Pennsylvania Transit Authority was accompanied by a graphic, bordered top and bottom by rails, titled "The SEPTA Hit List: If Your Train Is High Up on This List, It Is in Danger of Being Eliminated." Thirteen trains were listed in declining order of endangerment in the chart, each accompanied by the percentage of its costs covered by fares, its passengers per mile, and its loss per passenger mile.

The redesign won an award, but sent a number of the more conservative *Bulletin* readers into orbit. Some madman had got hold of their paper! Complaints flooded the *Bulletin*'s switchboard, and Ammerman later conceded that the redesign should have been eased in rather than unloaded on the *Bulletin*'s readers like a painter's drop cloth falling out a window.

The desperately struggling *Bulletin* didn't restrict its revitalization efforts to redesign. Investigative and interpretative reporters were hired and unleashed.

Typical stories these reporters produced included a front-page piece about a possible $58 million governmental subsidy to a member of the ultrarich Mellon family of Pittsburgh, and the revelation that Philadelphia's taxpayers had paid for a trip to Hawaii for officials of the city's police officers union.

Another story was headlined "Philadelphia's Arraignment Court—Justice in a Dirty Fishbowl."

On the theory that most people have attended high school at one time or another, one *Bulletin* reporter was enrolled undercover as a student in an average Philadelphia high school. He discovered, along with the dope-dealing he had expected to find, that the school days lasted only four and one-half hours, that no food was available at the school except candy bars sold by teachers, and that in some classes the students never received the textbooks promised them.

The paper also ran long, well-researched series on cancer research and on the lessons learned from the U.S. space program. At long last, the *Bulletin* was trying both to explain the complexities of modern life to its readers, and thoroughly to explore life's darker side.

The paper really hit its stride with a lengthy series charging that the jury that convicted former United Mine Workers president W. A. (Tony) Boyle didn't get all the facts before it convicted Boyle for the 1969 murder of Joseph A. (Jock) Yablonski and his wife and daughter. (Yablonski was the

white-knight reform candidate who had unsuccessfully challenged Boyle for the union presidency that year.)

The first installment of the series sprawled across three
fourths of the *Bulletin*'s front page and occupied almost four
full pages inside the paper; four reporters had spent eighteen
weeks crisscrossing the country with lie detectors to pin the
story down.

The paper demanded, in an editorial headlined "The Rail-
roading of Tony Boyle," that the ailing former union leader
be granted a new trial, and questioned the conduct of the
special prosecutor in the case. The prosecutor responded by
suing the *Bulletin* for $12 million and charging that the story
was aimed at helping the *Bulletin* escape "imminently
threatening financial collapse."

In a report released six weeks after the *Bulletin*'s series
ran, Pennsylvania's attorney general exonerated the special
prosecuter, declaring that there was "no support" for the
Bulletin's allegations of misconduct. The *Washington Post*
noted, however, that although "the *Bulletin* may have been
going down the tubes, it was attempting to go down in the
great tradition—battling for justice to the end, keeping the
authorities straight, righting wrongs, and keeping its dwin-
dling readership informed."

As the editorial that accompanied the Boyle series indicated, the *Bulletin*'s editorial page had begun to take strong
positions on local issues. It even asked readers to send in
their thoughts, negative or positive, on controversial issues
and people.

Still, the *Bulletin*'s losses continued to mount as Hayden
and Ammerman spent millions to improve it while advertising continued on its downhill run.

To make matters worse, in July 1980 the *Inquirer*'s circulation exceeded the *Bulletin*'s for the first time, and the

number of advertisers leaving the *Bulletin* for the *Inquirer* increased exponentially. Advertisers were following their modern newspaper advertising strategy, which was to put most of their ads in the top newspaper in each market.

The *Bulletin*'s losses increased dramatically. After dropping $8 million in 1979, it went on to lose $13 million in 1980 and $10 million in the first six months of 1981. Meanwhile, other Charter Media properties also were losing money, bringing the company's reported losses to $27 million during the second quarter of 1981.

This left the *Bulletin*'s fate in Mason's hands. Unfortunately for the newspaper, though, all Mason had ever been able to do with most of his media properties was buy them and watch their worth erode in spite of his efforts to improve them. None of his oil business magic seemed to rub off on them. In fact, even that seemed to be rubbing thin. The profits of Charter Company, Charter Media's parent, declined dramatically from their peak as the oil glut took hold.

When Charter Media had purchased the *Bulletin*, many observers worried about the stories or editorials an oil company might force a newspaper to run or to kill. Their concern turned out to be misplaced. Charter never interfered with the *Bulletin*'s editorial operations.

The real problem with linking the *Bulletin* to an oil firm was that the drop in oil prices, which under normal circumstances would have cut the *Bulletin*'s costs, and thus helped it, instead left Charter with less money to spend on the paper, and thus hurt it.

In a sense, after Charter took over the *Bulletin*, the fate of a major Philadelphia newspaper rested in the hands of such journalistic men of vision as Ayatollah Khomeini of Iran and President Muammar el-Quaddafi of Libya.

For a while, though, whatever Khomeini's motives, it looked as if the war he was waging with Iraq, and the destruction it was expected to wreak upon both countries' oil-producing capacity, would cause oil prices to rise, increase Charter's earnings, and help the *Bulletin*. As for its impact on Philadelphia, the Iran-Iraq war might as well have been taking place on Market Street, and the *Bulletin* wouldn't have been blamed for sending half its staff to cover it.

In any case, as a result of the decline in Charter's oil earnings, Charter Media had much less money to spend on the *Bulletin* or to invest in other media properties.

Partly as a result, and partly because of disagreements he said he was having with Mason, Eller left Charter Media six months after the company was founded. He took some of Charter Media's holdings with him but left the *Bulletin* where he found it: going down the drain in Philadelphia.

With Charter Company on a downswing, Mason and his executives couldn't see much sense in continuing to pour millions into the *Bulletin*, unless they got some help, and got it fast.

Publisher Hayden, taking his cue from publishers all over the world in this era—including Rupert Murdoch at the *Times* of London and both Joe Allbritton and Time, Inc. at the *Washington Star*—announced, in effect, that if Charter wouldn't pay, and the advertisers wouldn't pay, then the unions would have to pay. He announced that Charter would close the paper unless the unions agreed to layoffs and other concessions that would cut the *Bulletin*'s costs by $6 million a year.

Some observers wondered how a $6 million annual saving would give substantial succor to a paper losing $20 million a year, but hidden among the concessions Charter requested were numerous requests for changes in work rules and manning procedures that would have saved the paper millions more in years to come. Anyway, even the $6 million would have given Charter more time to turn the paper around.

In return for the sought-after concessions, Hayden promised to give the paper's employees 25 percent of any future *Bulletin* profits, a breathtakingly socialist concession for an American businessman to make. He also promised that Charter would invest $30 million in the *Bulletin* to make it profitable once again.

The unions were swayed less by the lure of future profits and the promise of further investment from Charter than by the stark alternative offered them: if they balked, they walked. They decided to give Charter what it wanted.

The *Bulletin* heralded the union concessions with an advertising and promotion blitz. A *Bulletin* radio advertising campaign began, featuring Pete Rose, then the Phillies star first basemen. A cashcard sweepstakes was begun. The paper announced it would spend $1.25 million to repaint, refurbish, and redecorate all its delivery trucks, newsstands, and coin boxes as well as buy new delivery trucks and open 240 new retail outlets. The *Bulletin*'s sports section was doubled in size and extra space was added for coverage of Atlantic City and for stories about personal money management.

Then, to attract the young people, the working women, the jocks, the computer nuts, and others who had discovered no compelling reason to read the *Bulletin* rather than the *Inquirer*, the paper instituted a series of weekly feature sections, including "Electronic Home," "Working Women," "Senior," "Participation Sports," "Single," and "Money and Leisure."

Each of these sections attempted to cover every aspect of whatever subject it dealt with from every possible angle, always with emphasis on involving the reader in the activity featured. For instance, a "Participation Sports" section might include a story about the World Bowling Cup Competition, a column entitled "What to Wear If Cold, Wet," a test of reader knowledge of sports terms, a calendar of future local participation-sports events, a "Sports Medicine" column entitled "Early to Bed Good Idea—If You're Tired," an "Outdoors" column, and a column listing the best local bowling scores sent in by readers. A typical "Single" section would contain stories such as "Church-Oriented Groups Preferred by Many Singles," "A Party for Parent and Kids," "Easing the Transition from Married to Single," a column on "Places Where People Meet People," a "Got-a-Question?" column, and a calendar for singles.

The paper's leisure section, called "Time Out," carried this principle to the nth degree. A typical "Time Out" section included a special-events column, an around-town column, an eating-out column, a nightwatch column, a "Poptalk" column, a pop-rock-jazz column, an auction column, a "Time-Out-for-Kids" column, and a health column. It also would include movie reviews, play reviews, and music-dance reviews, as well as a music-dance calendar, a fairs and festivals calendar, a "Fun and Games" calendar, an auctions calendar, an antiques calendar, and an arts calendar.

This was "user-friendly" journalism at its most elaborate. There wasn't the slightest chance that anyone interested in any of these subjects wouldn't be attracted by at least one of these articles, or feel compelled, somehow, to make use of or participate in the section.

Readers got into the act in another way as well. Along with the new sections, Hayden and Ammerman started a new edition of the *Bulletin*, a "Blue Streak" or late edition, which carried the final stock-market listings. After a short while, though, they became aware that the edition cost a lot more to publish than it gained in ad revenues. But when they stopped publishing it, so many influential business people complained about its demise that Hayden and Ammerman felt compelled to start publishing it again, whatever the cost.

The *Bulletin*'s new managers tried to build on their paper's strengths, and the *Bulletin* certainly had them. It knew Philadelphia, its traditions and its people, and was at home there. For years, it had covered traditional Philadelphia events and locations with respect and accuracy. The Mummer's Parade on New Year's Day, the Ninth Street Italian market, the soft mustard-covered pretzels that were sold outside the Phillies games all had their place in the *Bulletin*. It was accurate and respected and thorough and fair, and—years ago—had seemed even fairer when all there was to compare it with was the sometimes biased and self-serving *Inquirer* under Annenberg.

Under its new managers, with its new sections, its circulation began growing again, and the circulation gap between the *Bulletin* and the *Inquirer* actually began to close. If Hayden and Ammerman had been able not just to narrow the gap between the *Bulletin* and the *Inquirer* but to regain the circulation lead for their paper, many of the city's advertisers might well have returned to the *Bulletin* and the paper might have had a chance at survival.

The *Bulletin*'s promotional and editorial efforts, however, obscured an important part of Charter's agreement with the unions: that the *Bulletin* would have to meet certain circulation and advertising targets on its climb back to profitability if Charter was to continue to subsidize the paper. If the *Bulletin* was even to begin to meet those benchmarks, the competitive *Inquirer*, which had shown when it stripped Doonesbury from the *Bulletin* that it was in the Philadelphia newspaper wars to win, would have to restrain its lust for blood.

For a short while after the unions made their concessions to the *Bulletin*, it appeared that such restraint would not be forthcoming.

Knight-Ridder's chief Philadelphia executive, Sam McKeel, began telling people that the unions couldn't go around granting concessions to just one of Philadelphia's four papers and that he'd insist those same unions grant those same concessions to the *Inquirer* and *Daily News*.

McKeel knew, of course, that the unions, which had agreed to grant concessions to the obviously ailing *Bulletin* to save the jobs of their members there, were not about to agree to further salary cuts and layoffs to swell the treasuries of Knight-Ridder's Philadelphia properties, which had become profitmakers. Had McKeel insisted on this sort of equity, the only real choice for the unions would have been to withdraw the concessions they had granted the *Bulletin*, killing it on the spot. McKeel, though, said his only concern was that the concessions not work to the *Inquirer*'s disadvantage. In any case, it became obvious during 1981 that the union concessions weren't going to save the *Bulletin*, so McKeel never pressed his demands.

Almost as an afterthought, Knight-Ridder also rejected shortly thereafter a renewed Charter Company suggestion that the three papers link arms in a joint operating agreement. Charter, watching its money flow through the *Bulletin* and out to sea as 1981 ebbed, proposed again that the *Inquirer*, *Bulletin*, and *Daily News* publish jointly. The *Bulletin* still had 412,000 readers and 30 percent of the city's newspaper advertising, and capturing those readers and advertisers intact would have been a big prize for the aggressive Knight-Ridderites. But if the *Bulletin* died, Knight-Ridder would get all those advertisers and most of those readers anyway, without being forced to subsidize the *Bulletin*'s growing losses.

Knight-Ridder carefully and thoughtfully weighed on the one hand the possibility of unobstructed profits, and on the other hand the possibility of maintaining Philadelphia's tradition of competitive independent journalism—and snapped out a "no" before the petitioning *Bulletin* executives could give their names to the receptionist.

That was just about that for the poor old *Bulletin*. With the final bell approaching, all that remained was for the *Bulletin*'s strongest local ally to hit the canvas for good: Pulpy wasn't going to make it this time.

Pulpy Pierre Peladeau, who was paying the *Bulletin* to print his *Philadelphia Journal*, had not been able to attract the readers or advertisers he needed. The *Journal*'s circulation had dropped to 96,000 by 1980 and although Peladeau had said he could make it on 80,000, he was assuming a minimal level of advertising, which he didn't get. Advertisers tended to put most of their ads in the top newspaper in each market, and with the *Journal* fourth out of four, it got almost no ads.

Peladeau also shared an advertising problem with Rupert Murdoch and his *New York Post:* many of the people who read his paper were down-at-heel inner-city types who spent most of their money on necessities. It was the upscale, quiche-eating suburbanites with money to spend that the advertisers were after.

After four years gone and $15 million spent, Peladeau decided he couldn't go on without changing the rules of the game. He attempted to do exactly what the *Bulletin* had done, convince the unions to accept layoffs and wage cuts to save their jobs and save Peladeau $3 million annually.

With this extra breathing space, he would convert the *Journal* to an all-sports paper. Eliminating the nonsports news from the paper would reduce its size, allowing Peladeau to cut costs even further while holding onto most of the paper's readers, who didn't care what was happening outside the stadium anyway.

But like a merchant rejecting an out-of-towner's check, the same unions that had given the home-grown *Bulletin* what it wanted told Peladeau no, and in December 1981 the *Philadelphia Journal* folded. (Union resistance stemmed partly from an earlier crisis at the *Journal*, when Peladeau's executives had threatened to close the paper if the unions failed to come around but did not follow through on their threat.)

Pulpy Pierre could at least trundle on back to the North Woods, the source of all pulp. But he left the poor old *Bulletin* standing there naked, no longer covered by the lucrative *Journal* printing contract, awaiting the knives of the circling *Inquirer* and *Daily News*.

The *Bulletin* lasted only one month longer. The poor old paper was losing money and advertisements so fast it was virtually hemorrhaging, its blood obscuring the benchmarks Charter had carved out for it. No one was informing the paper's readers and advertisers about the goals Charter had set out for them. After losing $13 million in 1980, the *Bulletin* lost $22 million in 1981, even with the union concessions, and $3 million more in January 1982 alone. This month of exponentially increasing losses was the month the paper was supposed to meet its first benchmark. Charter Company announced that the game was over and the paper was for sale.

In the midst of selling its other media properties as well, Charter put the *Bulletin* on sale at a huge discount: no cash down, $10 million payable over five years, and $20 million more payable only if the new owners made a profit. Adding honey to the pot, the city of Philadelphia, eager to keep the *Bulletin* going and the paper's 1,900 employees employed, offered tax breaks and tax-exempt low-interest loans to any buyer who took the plunge. But the *Bulletin* was losing $100,000 a day and investors could think of more promising things to do with their money. No one stepped forward to embrace the old gray lady of Market Street, as the *Bulletin* had once affectionately been called. On January 29, 1982, the paper closed for good.

Shortly after the *Bulletin* died, it became obvious why Sam McKeel, by 1981, had felt he could do better without joining the *Bulletin* in a joint operating agreement. Three months after newspaper competition in Philadelphia ended, the *Inquirer's* daily circulation had grown from 420,000 to 574,000 and its Sunday circulation from 850,000 to 1,045,000. In addition, *Daily News* circulation grew by nearly 80,000 to 309,000. Ad linage also rose, and, Knight-Ridder executives gloated, the company's dual Philadelphia holdings might soon challenge San Jose, California, for the title of second-most profitable city in the Knight-Ridder empire.

The *Inquirer* also immediately snatched up the *Bulletin's* old comics, adding four full pages to its Sunday comics section in the process. With no competitor, Knight-Ridder felt free to raise the *Inquirer's* price to twenty-five cents per copy and increase ad rates.

This wasn't as greedy as it may have seemed, at least in the short run, for Knight-Ridder was now involved in an expensive scramble for the loyalty of former *Bulletin* readers. Knight-Ridder executives hustled around buying new buildings, new presses, and new delivery trucks to keep up with the virtual avalanche of new subscribers that threatened to bury them. The *Daily News* hired eight new reporters, opened suburban bureaus, added two sports columnists, a local columnist, a Washington columnist, a second op-ed page, nine news pages, and a business section.

The larger and more editorially ambitious *Inquirer* added fifty staffers; opened news bureaus in New Delhi, London, Cairo, and Nairobi to add to its bureaus already in operation in Rome and Bangkok, domestic bureaus in New Orleans and Boston to add to its existing domestic bureaus in New York, Chicago, Detroit, Los Angeles, and Houston; began a features section and a tabloid book section; and beefed up the rest of its coverage. Both papers grew in size by 20 percent.

The *Inquirer* also assigned twenty of its new reporters to the suburbs and immediately began weekly suburban news sections in addition to everything else. Its new young reporters on their way out to the suburbs soon clashed, however, with a horde of suburban publishers, editors, and reporters charging the other way, intent on capturing the 405,000 former *Bulletin* subscribers for themselves. The suburban papers began phone-soliciting every former *Bulletin* reader they could find, expanding their news pages, jumping from morning to afternoon publication, adding Sunday editions and columnists, lowering their prices, hiring former *Bulletin* circulation managers and newsboys, and distributing thousands of free copies of their own papers. One aggressive suburban newspaper chain even started a new paper in a suburban area thick with former *Bulletin* readers and hired a former *Bulletin* managing editor to run it.

Three of the most aggressive suburban papers immediately attempted to wrest from the somewhat overloaded *Inquirer* the exclusive rights that paper claimed to Peanuts, America's most popular comic strip. The three papers first went to court, asserting that losing Peanuts would cause them a serious setback in their "life and death" struggle with the *Inquirer* for suburban readership. While the judge considered their case, they appealed to the people with a "Free Snoopy" campaign, complete with front-page editorials and photos of a Snoopy doll peering out from behind an *Inquirer* as if from a cell. The court ruled in their favor.

As these good-humored sharks rushed to devour its remains, the defunct *Bulletin* sank into the depths of the past, taking with it the jobs of nineteen hundred Philadelphians and a competitive news source for a million more.

It also seemed to take with it the rest of Charter Company's media effort. During 1981 and 1982, the company sold most of its media holdings. For Mason and Charter, the media was the message, and the message was "Get Out!" Charter discovered that it was better at running oil refineries than trying an eleventh-hour rescue of a neglected newspaper fighting two tougher, smarter, and better-financed opponents. Indeed, the mandate of heaven seemed to have been lifted from Mason's entire operation (which eventually filed for bankruptcy). Later that year four top Charter Company executives were killed when a helicopter ferrying them from ancient Bellinahinch Castle, Mason's exclusive hotel on Ireland's rugged west coast, vanished and crashed, just like Philadelphia's last independent newspaper, and Charter's hopes of saving it.

CHAPTER FOUR

He Came to Do Good and He Did Well

The *Washington Star* Under Joe Allbritton

Crosby Noyes, Samuel Kauffmann, and associates bought the *Washington Star* in 1867, and made it into one of the most successful and respected daily newspapers in America. For generations it was a leading opinionmaker. Its editorials helped build and improve Washington, D.C. Its news columns were widely read. For a time, it carried more advertising than any other newspaper in the United States. It made money . . . for a long time.

The Kauffmann and Noyes families appreciated the money they made and the social position they maintained as a result of owning what was for many years the capital's dominant newspaper. They also were interested, however, in their children's—and grandchildren's—future, not as federal bureaucrats but as reporters and editors on the *Washington Star.* Filial rebellion had always been rare among the Kauffmanns and Noyeses. As the generations rolled on, most descendants gladly took their preordained places on the *Star* staff, determined to live out their professional lives on the newspapers and pass their positions on to their progeny.

Like any staffers employed on the basis of kinship rather than inherent skills, the hired relatives sometimes turned out to be prodigiously skilled at their work, and sometimes not. One hired relative, Newbold Noyes, so impressed *Star* columnist Mary McGrory that she stayed on at the newspaper out of loyalty to Noyes long after the *Star* had fallen from its peak, and despite attractive offers from the *Washington Post.*

Keeping their relatives on the payroll was fine for the Kauffmanns and Noyeses and, in some cases, fine for the *Star.* But it was the darkest iniquity as far as the paper's ambitious reporters were concerned. Reporting was and is a young person's game. Most young reporters eventually tire of covering press conferences—or even searching out injustice—and begin to think about their futures. Some opt for public relations or teaching or writing or politics, but many want to be editors. At the *Star* unless such reporters were named Noyes or Kauffmann, they were less likely to rise to the highest editorial ranks than those who were. Such stalwarts as Haynes Johnson and David Broder began a migration to the *Post* when they saw their upward mobility blocked at the *Star.* Others followed. (Eventually, when it became obvious that the *Star* was sinking and the *Post* was rising, the migration became a stampede. In 1975 the *Star's* own "Ear" column carried this self-mocking comment: "A *Washington Post* elevator fell two stories today. Twelve *Washington Star* reporters [résumés presumably in hand] were injured.")

The *Star's* owners, however, were so secure in their hold on the paper and so satisfied with what they assumed to be their unassailable position in the capital that they failed to take seriously the powerful offensive launched against them by the *Post.*

Not that the *Post's* managers had ever hidden their intentions, even in the early days. In fact, as far back as 1889 they blared them from the rooftops, hiring the one and only John Philip Sousa to write the "Washington Post March" to launch their long campaign to establish the *Post*'s preeminence over all other Washington dailies.

The *Star*'s owners tapped their feet, listened to the music, and decided to wait and see. Wait and see seemed a sensible policy at the time, and for many years thereafter. Even in the early 1950s, after decades of steady competition from the *Post*, the *Star*, with a circulation of a quarter million, was America's fifth largest daily and the capital's dominant newspaper.

At about this time, the *Post*'s owners realized that, to make any progress, they would have to buy out their morning competition. Desire meshed with opportunity when the *Washington Times-Herald*, the *Post*'s morning competitor, went on the auction block in 1954. The *Star*'s owners, basking in the afternoon sun, could have purchased the *Times-Herald*, but chose not to. From the heights of the *Star*'s dominance, the owners saw no reason to move to the morning from what seemed to be a secure afternoon throne nor any reason to buy a morning paper. Even if the *Post* bought and closed the *Times-Herald*, the *Star*'s owners said, *Times-Herald* readers would end up at the *Star*, along with everyone else in Washington. So they let the *Post* absorb the dying paper.

The *Post*'s owners, showing their corporate cunning, and honing the razor's edge with which the paper later would cut down a president, did not change the paper's name to the *Washington Post–Times-Herald*. They had the decency, and the corporate smarts, to inter the dead newspaper and let it rest in peace, except for a memorial mention in very small print under the huge letters that spelled out *"Washington Post"* on the *Post*'s masthead. These letters became smaller and smaller over the years and eventually disappeared. A subterranean journalistic principle was at work. Those papers that bought out the competition, took it to the alley and killed it, keeping most of the blood off the front windows, are now America's leading newspapers, morning or afternoon. Those that insisted on displaying the bloody remains are dead or dying themselves.

Not long after the *Post* swallowed the *Times-Herald*, the *Star*'s owners knew something was up. It turned out to be their number.

The *Post* began gaining ads and readers while the *Star* languished. Afternoon newspaper disease gave the *Post* a big assist, but so did the *Star*'s owners, who had run out of ideas that would improve their paper or its financial fortunes. (One analyst contends that during the 1950s and 1960s, the *Star* used more daily Associated Press copy than any other American newspaper, not exactly a sign of a creative journalistic imagination at work.)

In 1972, with its ad linage and circulation falling rapidly, the *Star* made a desperate move: it bought its competition, the afternoon *Washington Daily News*, and became the *Star-News*. Years before, such a move might have returned the *Star* to preeminence, but by 1972 the *Star* was so firmly in the clutches of afternoon newspaper disease that purchasing the sick afternoon *Daily News* did nothing to alleviate its own illness. With suburban and upscale readers drifting away, a growing percentage of its remaining readership consisted of the relatively downscale residents of the District of Columbia and downtown office workers who bought it on the newsstands. These were not the flossy, upscale advertisers' darlings who motored off to the suburbs each evening.

By the mid-1970s the Kauffmans and Noyeses had put the *Star* up for sale.

Even in the throes of its illness, however, the *Star* could still attract suitors, and among its gentlemen callers were two of our era's most picturesque movers and shakers: a publisher who may have been a South African agent, and a flamboyant Texas banker and funeral-home owner, Joseph L. Allbritton, owner of Pierce Brothers Inc., a California mortuary chain, and several other businesses.

Allbritton was the perfect buyer for the *Star-News.* No one knew the profits of both life and death as well as he. When he bought Pierce Brothers in 1958, he discovered that it sold life insurance on the side. He built up that end of the business into the Pierce National Life Insurance Company, keeping the mortuary operation intact. While you lived, you paid premiums to Allbritton; when you died, you paid funeral costs to Allbritton. Having founded his fortune this way, he went on to buy and then sell the Houston Bank and Trust Company, building his estimated worth to $100 million. He approached the moribund *Washington Star-News* with money in hand.

Despite his somewhat unorthodox background and the ten-gallon hat and string tie he occasionally sported, Allbritton was not the most interesting suitor to approach the *Star-News.*

In a city in which so many of America's big decisions were made, any major newspaper for sale was bound to attract at least one special-interest group seeking to disguise its special pleadings.

Such a suitor was the Republic of South Africa, a fabulously rich country in which five million whites maintain a racist dominion over twenty-three million blacks. Although a number of its policies, including its racial policies, are officially disapproved of by the United States government, the South African government is supported by many Americans as anticommunist (and, perhaps, as racist). No other country was better financed, or more motivated, to buy a Washington newspaper and use it to nudge the U.S. government closer to friendship.

But the South Africans would have to buy the *Star-News* secretly, and to do so they would have to find a believable U.S. front man. A likely target for their efforts was John McGoff, head of the now defunct Panax Corporation, owner of sixty-five weekly newspapers and six dailies in the Midwest and Southwest.

McGoff is a very conservative Republican who wanted his sometimes extreme views reflected in the news columns as well as in the editorial columns of his newspapers. In 1977, for instance, editors of two Michigan papers left Panax after Panax headquarters ordered them to run two dubious stories about President Jimmy Carter.

One of the stories suggested that Carter encouraged sexual promiscuity among male White House staff members. The other reported that the president was grooming Mrs. Carter for a run at the vice presidency.

Both stories were written by George Bernard, Panax's New York bureau chief, who previously had worked for a scandal sheet, the *National Enquirer*. One of the Panax editors refused to run the stories and was fired; the other refused to run one story, rewrote the other, and resigned. From then on, word was, any story marked "MG" meant "McGoff" or "Must Go."

The South Africans must have decided that this was the sort of publisher they wanted running their Washington newspaper, if they could get their hands on one. Why waste time with namby-pambies?

McGoff has denied being a front or an agent for anyone, but in 1978 an official South African government commission reported that McGoff was provided with more than $11.5 million from a secret South African propaganda fund during his attempt to purchase the *Star.* When that deal fell through, the commission reportedly said, McGoff used more than $5 million of the money to buy into the *Sacramento Union.* (In 1983 an investigation by the U.S. Securities and Exchange Commission aimed at discovering if McGoff violated the law by using South African government funds to purchase interests in American newspapers ended in a stalemate: McGoff neither admitted nor denied any wrongdoing in the past with regard to SEC regulations, but agreed not to violate SEC rules in the future.)

Unfortunately for McGoff, the Kauffmanns and Noyeses, although unaware of McGoff's alleged South African connection, knew of the controversy surrounding him. They weren't about to turn over their only newspaper, a precious family heirloom, to such a controversial publisher. Furthermore, without knowing about McGoff's alleged South African funds, the Kauffmanns and Noyeses didn't believe the Michigan-based publisher had the wherewithal to buy the *Star.* They rejected his bid.

As the South African commission reported, McGoff went on to buy an interest in the *Sacramento Union,* but it's hard to believe the South Africans weren't disappointed by this lowering of sights. California is a big and important state, but did the issues the *Union* might influence—the state budget surplus, the Santa Barbara oil spills—really appear all that vital in Pretoria? (McGoff later sold his interest in the *Union.*)

Meanwhile, back in D.C., the Texas banker was still trying to buy the *Star-News.*

Allbritton wanted to emerge from the relative anonymity of this great nation's legion of rich businessmen and take his place in the sunlight as an influential Washington newspaper publisher. But Allbritton remained a down-home hustler with genius for making money and there was no evidence lightning had struck him on the road to Washington. He knew he wasn't going to make much money running an afternoon newspaper in the District of Columbia, where white-collar suburbanites tend to read morning newspapers and the inner-city poor aren't attractive to advertisers. Moreover, he knew the morning paper he'd be competing against would be journalism's new god, the *Washington Post,* at the height of its triumph, with both Woodward and Bernstein still on the roster and Janet Cooke not yet hired.

Allbritton wouldn't even have bothered with the *Star-News,* in fact, were it not for an act its owners had committed in the paper's late middle age, when they saw only declining years ahead of it and decided to give it one last fling with a sexy young industry—television—that might be able to support it in its dotage.

So inspired, the Kauffmanns and the Noyeses had purchased three radio and television stations in Washington and three more in Virginia and South Carolina. TV and radio had proven so frisky that by the time Allbritton came along the stations the *Star-News* had acquired in an Indian summer gambol threatened to dwarf it financially.

Excruciatingly aware of this, Allbritton made it clear early on that he wouldn't purchase the *Star-News* were he not allowed to purchase the radio and television stations as well. The Kauffmanns and Noyeses would rather have sold the money-losing *Star* and held onto their moneymaking radio and TV stations, but the profligate *Star* was losing more than the radio and TV stations were producing in profits. Rather than stand there helplessly watching their century-old fortune slip away, the old families yielded to the Texas banker and sold him the *Star* and the stations.

During the turmoil surrounding Allbritton's purchase of the paper, some disquieted staff members saw him before his time, or thought they did. Allbritton dressed like a Lower Manhattan business executive on most occasions but the *Star* staff knew him only by reputation. One day during this period two men wearing Stetsons, vests, and cowboy boots entered the newsroom. All work stopped. The two men strode bowleggedly through the room and headed for the city editor's desk, looking neither to the right nor to the left. All eyes fastened upon them. The city editor looked up, saw the men coming, and gulped. When they reached his desk, he managed to stammer, "Can I help you?" When the men announced they were from the rodeo and wanted some publicity everyone went back to work.

Allbritton was no rodeo star, but he was almost hogtied during his maneuvers to purchase the *Star* by a Federal Communications Commission policy forbidding one person from buying newspaper and broadcast outlets in the same market. He argued that he needed the revenue from the stations to maintain the *Star-News* and thus maintain newspaper competition in D.C. Wasn't media competition the goal of FCC policy? The FCC reaffirmed its policy on single ownership, but gave Allbritton three years to sell off either the *Star* or the stations, rather than require him to do so immediately.

Three years was all Allbritton needed. He knew—from experience—the profits that could be made from holding on, even briefly. After graduating from law school in 1949, he had purchased 400 acres of Houston real estate for $350 an acre, 10 percent down. The land doubled in value in one year and by 1976 was worth $30,000 an acre.

A man who had so enriched himself from mere real estate could only dream of the total profits to be made from briefly owning radio and TV stations in and around the capital of the most video-conscious nation on earth.

While the stations were producing $4 million a year in profits, however, the *Star-News* was losing $5 million a year. Allbritton saw only one immediate solution to such a situation: cut costs at the newspaper. Three months after he took over the management of the *Star* in 1974, Allbritton threatened to lay off two hundred employees or shut the paper. To show he was serious, he halted newsprint deliveries to the *Star* and let its supply of the precious commodity dwindle to two days' worth.

The first reaction came from the members of the paper's Newspaper Guild, those tough, cynical *Star-News* reporters, editors, and commercial employees who became pliant pussycats when Allbritton threatened to close their paper or fire their comrades.

To avoid layoffs, they voted to work a four-day week for four days' pay. This was a unique and touching moment in journalism. No other news staff had made such a move before and none has done so since, not even on afternoon newspapers in worse trouble than the *Star-News* (although other *Star* unions took other moves to avoid layoffs). The eventual death of the *Star-News* in spite of its guild members' self-sacrifice discouraged other guild units from making similar concessions.

The first round of cuts was easy, but, only a year later, Allbritton asked all *Star* employees to forgo their scheduled pay increases for a year (although, to sweeten the bitter pill, he allowed the guild members to return to a five-day week for five days' pay).

The unions' reaction to these new demands might have been a lot tougher had not a grand dame across town heard some loud clanging from her pressroom. What Katharine Graham, publisher of the *Washington Post*, heard was the sound of some of the *Post*'s pressmen sabotaging her presses as they went out on strike. As it turned out, they not only went out on strike, they went out for good. Even though the *Post* building was ringed with picketers, Graham's paper missed only one day of publication. Helicopters flew the plates for each page high over the picketers to the printing plants of cooperative suburban newspapers, and the *Post* pulled itself back together, minus the absent unionists. (The aid these suburban dailies provided at the *Post*'s moment of crisis cemented locally an alliance that had been growing up naturally all around the country between the big-city morning dailies and the suburban papers, mostly evenings.)

Graham's triumph frightened the D.C. newspaper unions and convinced most of them to agree to Allbritton's demands. The unions were so docile, in fact, that at one negotiating session a Teamsters' representative sang "Que Sera, Sera" throughout the meeting. At whatever palatial estate the former publishers of afternoon newspapers may choose to gather, this gesture should be recalled with champagne and backslapping. It is doubtful that future demands for salary cuts and layoffs at other newspapers will ever again be met with such meekness.

Dr. Johnson once said that remarriage is the triumph of hope over experience. So, too, are union sacrifices to publishers who claim they'll be forced to close shop if sacrifices aren't forthcoming. It's likely, therefore, that unions will go on accepting wage cuts or forgoing wage increases, meekly or not, in attempts to save their jobs, although none of the afternoon newspapers at which such sacrifices have been made has long survived thereafter.

Allbritton was very successful with his unions, but budget cutting could be pushed only so far. As Allbritton himself often said, "You can't save yourself into prosperity." He had to make the *Star-News* a moneymaker. To do that, he had to turn it into a paper that would attract readers and, eventually, advertisers.

He looked around for a man who would make the *Star* into the paper he wanted it to be. (Although Allbritton had hinted that the Kauffmann and Noyes reporters and executives would stay on in their *Star* jobs after he took over, that idea dried at about the same speed as the ink on the purchase contract. He later said he had fired all but one of them and kept that one around to remind him of how things had once been.)

With a Texas millionaire's luck, Allbritton soon found his man: James G. Bellows, who had started *New York* magazine as the *New York Herald Tribune*'s Sunday supplement. Although the *Herald Tribune* had died, *New York* magazine had prospered mightily as an independent, under Clay Felker, with its upscale offerings of high-class gossip and consumer features.

Bellows had moved on to redesign the feature sections of the *Los Angeles Times*, but the *Times* could hardly boast of the scrappy competitive *Front Page* atmosphere in which Bellows thrived. Its hushed, well-appointed newsroom and soft-spoken, well-dressed, upper middle-class employees, most with long tenure at the firm, gave it the soporific air of a long-established insurance company. Bellows called it "a velvet coffin."

Destined to become a major hero of the War in the Afternoon, Bellows loved to fight, and he was getting itchy for some knuckle-bruising. He already had fought the *New York Times*, the nation's best newspaper, the *New York Daily News*, its largest, and the *New York Post*, one of its most liberal. In the survival of *New York* magazine, he had come away with a fine reputation and a solid victory. Allbritton appointed Bellows editor of the *Star-News*.

Now Bellows had to decide how to improve the *Star-News*. He could compete with the *Post* by hiring hundreds of highly skilled, highly paid reporters, giving them the time and the expense accounts to produce high-quality journalism, and producing a paper thick enough to accommodate what they wrote. He could, in other words, make the *Star-News* into a second *Post* and attempt to supplant the *Post* in its readers' affections or hope people would read both. In a town like Washington, with its addiction to news, they just might. Some Washingtonians read both the *Post* and the *New York Times* every day, putting themselves among the nation's major consumers of newsprint. But competing with the *Post* that way would have cost millions of dollars annually.

Bellows decided that the best way to compete with the *Post* was by flashing, sizzling, analyzing, and rumormongering, by producing a thin, easily read paper that would dance inexpensively and light-footedly around the somewhat ponderous *Post*. He would give *Star-News* readers something to think about and something to laugh at without forcing the *Star-News* to spend the millions necessary to bring those readers a second *Post* every afternoon.

Doing it that way would also get the *Star* talked about, which was, Bellows thought, the surest way to attract readers in a closely knit town like Washington.

As part of this effort, Bellows attempted to build the *Star* into the king of the "why" and the "who." Larger-than-life national and international celebrities stalked Washington's drawing rooms, making the city a fascinating place to live. Bellows was determined to capture their comings and goings, the rumors that surrounded them, their peccadilloes, and their embarrassments. A gossip column, "Ear," quickly became the hallmark of the new *Star*. Written by *Star* staffers Diana McLellan and Louise Lague at the beginning and later by McLellan on her own, "Ear" poked irreverent fun at the love lives of public figures, taking special pleasure in razzing *Washington Post* executive editor Ben Bradlee and his room-mate and star reporter Sally Quinn. (They since have married.) In true gossip-column style, "Ear" referred to the *Post* as the "O.P." (for "Other Paper") and called Bradlee and Quinn the "Fun Couple."

"Ear" was part of Bellows' general strategy of, in his words, "getting the *Post* into the ring with us. We were David and they were Goliath." The *Star* had to work to make people notice that it was competing with the *Post*, and if annoying Ben and Sally did the trick, so much the better. "Ear" also allowed *Star* readers to feel superior to the glowing celebrities and political heavyweights the column tweaked and tittered at. Moreover, it allowed the glowing celebrities and political heavyweights to tweak and titter at each other. They did so with delight, flooding "Ear" with juicy items.

"Ear hears," the column reported, "that while superhost Ardeshir Zahedi may be great in a crowd, he's had at least one smoky moment in the snugly duo department. Seems he drew a lovely young thing into the embassy drawing room and tried to light a cozy fire. Alas, the servants had closed the flue and tossed candle ends onto the hearth and the pair ended up coughing instead of cooing. Ear respects men for their perfections, but adores them for their endearing little slips."

On another occasion, "Ear was shocked to find out what some congressional wives are giving their husbands for Christmas compared to what they're giving themselves. Four of them chipped in to buy a $1,000 catered dinner in a chartered jet over the city of their choice, hubbies not invited. But nearly 100 women bought Hortensia of Foxhall Square's Executive Christmas Stocking, a burlap affair stuffed with a Frisbee, a tic-tac-toe ball, a beanbag, some marbles, lollipops, and peanuts, for $5.50. Ear's source wouldn't say who bought the stockings, but prophesied they'd be all over the Hill."

Even the highest were not immune. "A non-French speaker at the all-French 'Mayflower' performance last week amused himself by counting the number of times Chief Justice Warren Burger, sharing a box with the French ambassador, yawned, and reported the total to Ear: 12."

Another Bellows innovation, "Gobbledygook," took the same tack. Like a similar column in *Washington Monthly*, it mocked the high and mighty by putting their most impenetrable memos on display. Both columns also encouraged reader participation and thus reader interest. The *Star* paid $5 or $10 for each memo sent to "Gobbledygook," and was flooded with hundreds.

Still another Bellows touch, a front-page interview column called "Q and A," treated *Star* readers to verbatim exchanges between *Star* reporters and such luminaries as Abdulrahman S. al-Alegi, the Kuwaiti minister of finance; Wendy Helander, an eighteen-year-old disciple of Rev. Sun Myung Moon; and Charles Miller, captain of the freighter *Mayaguez*, which had been captured by Cambodian forces. The column created a stir when, early on, it featured an interview with Goliath's brain, Katharine Graham.

Also, on the theory that one good writer is cheaper than one hundred new reporters and, if famous enough, might attract just as much attention, Bellows began a "Writer-in-Residence" program. This brought big-name scribes like Jimmy Breslin, Dick Schaap, Gloria Steinem, Tom Wolfe, and Gay Talese to the *Star* and to Washington for six-week stints, giving the writers the Washington exposure they wanted and attracting even more attention to the paper.

Knowing that the *Star*, as an afternoon paper, would constantly be beaten by the *Post* on daily stories, Bellows also instituted a daily *Star* feature called "In Focus," a long front-page article on a topic unrelated to the day's events. Among the subjects "In Focus" covered: the difficulties parents have purchasing toys that won't turn their kids into racists, sexists, or warmongers.

The *Star*'s general news coverage responded to the cues provided by these columns: lively features and long analytical pieces became the rule. Reporters on afternoon newspapers, and most of their readers as well, already knew the news of the day from reading the morning papers. Bellows wanted his reporters to write about why it had happened. Finding out why was well within their grasp, since their afternoon or late morning deadlines gave them an excellent chance of reaching the local philosophers and analysts at their workplaces. To conduct similar interviews, reporters for morning newspapers occasionally were reduced to tracking down such people at late-night parties, then eliciting their wisdom in the midst of a drunken revel, an always time-consuming, often unprofitable, and usually inefficient procedure.

Features aside, Bellows wanted the *Star-News* to compete head on with the *Post* in a least one area, local news. He expanded the *Star-News'* local coverage to equal the space allocated to local news by the *Post*. Meanwhile, he closed all the *Star-News'* foreign bureaus. This meant, of course, that far more of the *Star-News* than of the *Post* was devoted to local news, but meeting the *Post* on an equal basis somewhere, somehow, was exactly what Bellows had in mind.

Then Bellows dropped the *"News"* from the *Star-News* logo in an effort to remove his paper from the battalion of lost newspapers with names like *World Journal Tribune* and

News-Call-Bulletin and to join it with such stalwarts as the *New York Times*, the *Los Angeles Times*, and the *Chicago Tribune*.

The new *Star* was a lively alternative to the *Post*. And best of all, from Allbritton's point of view, was how cheap it was, at least compared with the cost of trying to compete against the *Post* on all fronts. The *Star's* new approach allowed Allbritton to argue that such spending would have been not only impossible, but also redundant and unnecessary. When Allbritton finally sold the *Star*, the *Post* had twice as many reporters as the *Star* (432 to 207) and more than twice the *Star's* editorial budget ($20 million to $8.6 million).

The new *Star* was lively and inexpensive, but it failed to attract the readers and advertisers it needed to stay alive. Its circulation and its ad content increased briefly during the *Post* strike. A few thousand additional readers picked it up to see what the fuss was all about and a few thousand who had been thinking of canceling had second thoughts for a few months.

But the *Post* expanded its feature and its television coverage, and continued its relentless delivery of all the news a person could read in newspaper, magazine, column, and Sunday supplement form.

Many people decided that reading the *Star* was equivalent to reading a supplement to a supplement and stopped it altogether, and circulation began to decline once again. *Star* circulation never had increased enough to encourage any substantial amount of new advertising, which is what the *Star* needed even more than it needed new readers. New readers only drove up its already exorbitant newsprint and delivery bills; new ads meant new money.

Meanwhile, all the credit Bellows was getting began to grate on Allbritton. Allbritton wanted to be a power in Washington, which, to a certain extent, he had become, but Bellows was getting too much ink.

"I made him," Allbritton complained of Bellows. "People talk like I hired Michelangelo to paint a barn. Well, I took someone who was painting barns and gave him the Sistine Chapel."

Allbritton was given to exaggeration, but comparing Bellows' former employers, the once mighty *New York Herald Tribune* and the still mighty *Los Angeles Times*, to barns, while comparing the *Washington Star* to the Sistine Chapel, showed to what extent jealousy had momentarily twisted Allbritton's judgment.

Although the two men remained, and remain, good friends, friction began to develop between them. Bellows wasn't just stealing the glory; he was standing in the way of Allbritton's kingmaking ambitions.

In 1976 President Ford was running against Ronald Reagan for the Republican presidential nomination. If Allbritton assisted him in a way everyone would notice, and Ford won both the nomination and the election, Allbritton would be the roaring lion of the new administration, a true press lord.

On July 4 of that year, the president invited Allbritton and a number of other Washington notables over to watch the Independence Day fireworks from the White House balcony. A short while later Allbritton visited the *Star* newsroom, gave the night man an editorial Allbritton had written endorsing Ford for renomination, and told him to run it on the front page the next day.

The night man called Bellows, who confronted Allbritton and insisted that the editorial should be written by one of the paper's regular editorial writers and should run on the editorial page, not the front page.

Look at it from Allbritton's point of view: he had invested

millions of his own money in a Washington daily. For the money involved, he probably could have built another Sistine Chapel. Then he had given a guy who had gone down with the *Herald Tribune* his big chance in the capital and what does the guy do? Refuses to let Allbritton run, on his own front page, an editorial that might have cemented his status in Washington for years to come. Did Bellows think he owned the place? As Allbritton said later, "If I tell my bank clerks to give out $2 bills only, they'll give out $2 bills only, until I tell them to stop. But if I go into the newsroom and tell them to do something, they won't do it." The pro-Ford editorial, written by a *Star* editorial writer, ran on the editorial page.

This incident made Allbritton more than a little nervous that Bellows, and his fellow newsroom denizens, might, through what Allbritton perceived as their disobedience, torpedo his Washington social status. A *Star* reporter had written a profile of Katharine Graham that the *Star* was planning to run as part of its coverage of the *Post*'s one hundredth anniversary. This was fine in principle with Allbritton, but the profile explored the tragedies in Graham's life as well as the triumphs, and Allbritton knew he was unlikely to gain entrée to the most trendy Washington salons, or make himself a well-liked and powerful figure in the capital, by nettling "The Most Powerful Woman in America," "The New Catherine the Great," Katharine Graham, publisher of the *Washington Post*.

He asked Bellows to agree not to publish the profile in the *Star* without checking with Allbritton first. Bellows agreed, and the Graham profile wasn't printed until after Allbritton no longer owned the *Star*.

But Bellows' most heinous sin, in Allbritton's eyes, was his failure to make the *Star* pay. After a brief spurt of black ink, the paper began to lose money again, Allbritton's money. Allbritton brought in a new president for the Star Company, James Smith, and told him to cut costs. "I'd like to cut back 50 percent if I could still produce a quality newspaper," Allbritton remarked.

Bellows said the new president ordered ads put on page 3, previously sacrosanct. Bellows saw this as the beginning of the end of his upgrading of the news and editorial part of the paper.

"The reader was going to get screwed," he said. He protested to the new president, and then to Allbritton, but both stood firm.

So Bellows in 1977 left for the *Los Angeles Herald Examiner*, whose publisher, the Hearst Corporation, was certainly more familiar with the ups and downs of newspaper publishing than Allbritton was. Before Bellows left town, though, Allbritton gave Bellows a Cadillac, to show there were no hard feelings. The Cadillac replaced the pink Thunderbird Bellows had driven as his company car at the "look-at-me" *Star*.

Then Allbritton returned grumpily to his ledger books and his cost-cutting. The FCC had given him three years to sell either the *Star* or its broadcast stations, and the end of the three-year period was approaching. Many expected Allbritton merely to close the *Star* and be done with it, but they were underestimating his financial genius and his sure-footed timing. He had an idea that something nice lay waiting for him just around the next bend, and he was right. There, cash in hand, stood Time, Incorporated.

Time, Inc. was looking around for new publishing properties, and it was only natural that its eye should fall on a newspaper published in a national and international center such as Washington, D.C.

Time saw itself, after all, not as a local or regional publisher, but as a national and international publisher, and a very successful one at that. Time's top executives felt that in their hands the *Star* could be made to reflect Washington's greatness and its position at the center of a national and worldwide system. Time also wanted to preserve a second newspaper voice in the nation's capital, its executives said.

Romance was also involved. Several of Time's highest executives were former newspapermen, who remembered, with visions colored pastel by the passage of years, the alleged romance of newspapering. Journalism in the nation's capital, moreover, seemed twice as romantic as journalism in Chicago's suburbs, the location of Time's only other newspaper holdings.

A financial angle also existed. Not long after Time, Inc. agreed to buy the *Star* for $16 million, the Times Mirror Company of Los Angeles purchased the *Hartford Courant* for $106 million. Even if Time spent millions on the *Star*, if it actually managed to save the paper and bring it to the breakeven point or above, it would own a Washington newspaper. But if the Times Mirror Co. made a gigantic success of the *Courant*, it would still own only a Connecticut newspaper.

Twice before, Time had considered purchasing the *Star*. In 1968, Time executives Murray Gart and Otto Fuerbringer had lunched with *Star* czar Jack Kauffmann in Washington's Jockey Club and suggested that he sell them his newspaper. Kauffmann refused. In 1974, with the *Star* definitely on the market, Time considered making another offer. But the paper was in poor financial shape and there were all those Kauffmanns and Noyeses on the payroll. Though Time executives felt they would have to let most of them go, they feared a fuss. But Allbritton, rich and influential as he was, was not in the same league as Time, Inc., publisher of *Time, Fortune,*

Sports Illustrated, People, and *Money,* and owner of the Book-of-the-Month Club, Home Box Office, and the Pioneer Press Newspapers. He could get away with a lot more than Time could without causing the slightest public outcry. After Allbritton fired the relatives at the *Star,* making the paper much more attractive, Time in 1978 decided to give the *Star* a try.

Well heeled and supremely confident, Time's executives descended upon the beleaguered *Star.* They paid Allbritton for the paper and left him his TV and radio stations. Allbritton could have stuffed million-dollar stock certificates in his mouth to keep from laughing, chewed 'em up and gulped 'em down, and never have noticed the loss.

After the dust had settled, the details of his financial triumph emerged. He had paid more than $35 million to acquire the *Star* and the stations. He paid about $30 million to underwrite the *Star's* losses. But aside from the $16 million Time, Inc. paid him, the cagey Allbritton had sold the *Star's* radio stations for $16.6 million. The TV stations he retained—in Washington, Virginia, and South Carolina—had grown in worth to $103 million. Allbritton's total profit on the buying and selling of the *Star* and its broadcast stations: $70 million.

To add to it all, two years before he sold the *Star,* Allbritton had again pressured the newspaper's unions, this time forcing them to agree to the layoffs of two hundred *Star* employees and a one-year freeze on wage increases, moves expected to save the paper $6 million a year. (Allbritton coupled this demand with a promise to provide the paper with $6 million in new capital.) Future labor historians will note with wonder the sacrifices the *Star's* labor unions accepted to enable Allbritton to walk away from the paper with $70 million instead of $58 million in pure profit.

In dollar terms, Allbritton had done better with the *Star* than he had done with Pierce Brothers Mortuaries. But the paper seemed about as dead as Pierce Brothers' customers, unless Time, Inc., the company with the Midas touch, could defy the dread afternoon newspaper disease and bring the *Star* once more to life.

CHAPTER FIVE

A Flawed Attempt

The *Washington Star* Under Time, Inc.

As the new owner of the *Washington Star*, Time, Inc.'s response to the paper's continuing monthly losses was the same as Allbritton's had been: cut, cut, cut. In the recent past, on three different occasions, the unions had panicked in the face of Allbritton's threats and yielded up their bounty. Now the new management decided it would have a go at the same game. But Allbritton had cowed the *Star*'s unions so successfully that Time could not claim the paper's employees were earning too much.

Time could, and did, state that a whole series of union work rules, embedded in the paper's contracts with its unions, would prevent the company from making a profit on the *Star* no matter what it did. Delivery routes, for instance, could not be altered without union agreement, and the *Star*'s new management wanted to alter many of them.

So Time demanded that such matters be returned to its control. If agreements could be worked out with each of the sixteen unions at the *Star*, Time said, it would invest $60 million in its newly purchased paper. If the unions refused, Time said, it would close the paper at the end of 1978.

Such threats weren't very original. Announcing that the

plant would close down if the workers didn't cough up had become a principal management technique of the recessionary late 1970s. But the *Star*'s typographers, at least, were getting a little tired of taking the fall. A few more rounds of "Let's pretend we're dead" and they wouldn't have to pretend. The typographers refused to give Time, Inc. what it wanted and then sued to prevent the company from closing the *Star.*

Time wasn't going to put up with this sort of thing. George Hoyt, newly appointed publisher of the *Star*, was called to the stand. He told the judge that he had the *Star*'s signed declaration of bankruptcy in his pocket. If the typographers didn't do what Time wanted, Hoyt said, he was going to walk over to the clerk's office as soon as he left the courtroom and file the declaration, ending the story of the *Washington Star* then and there. After all, Time hardly needed an afternoon rag in the District of Columbia to keep its coffers filled.

The judge told both sides to go back and negotiate some more. The typographers, however, had seen exactly what they were up against. They also knew that if they refused to go along with Time, the other unions would hold them responsible for the demise of the *Star* and the layoff of all its employees. They backed down—and Time got what it wanted.

Time had beaten down the unions—"We chose to be raped instead of murdered," one union official said—but now it had to beat the *Washington Post*, not so easy a task.

Murray Gart, head of Time-Life News Service, was appointed editor of the *Washington Star.* He argued that newspaper readers in Washington, D.C., knew too much about what newsmakers and reporters thought about events and too little about what actually took place. He clamped down on attempts by *Star* reporters to interpret events, in

Gart's words, as "broadly and facilely" as they had in the past. Gart also restricted the writing of investigative articles to those reporters he thought qualified to do so. (Some of Gart's reporters said he was against investigative and analytical reporting in general.)

He expanded the size of the *Star* editorial staff, increasing the number of stories written for the paper, and began to run stories filed specially for the *Star* by Time's large corps of foreign and domestic correspondents. He also insisted that the *Star*, physically a much smaller paper than the *Post*, attempt to cover many of the stories the *Post* covered. (After all, if the *Post* had the story, *Star* readers would see it in the *Post* or hear it on radio or TV, and would lose confidence in the *Star* if they didn't see it there as well.) Reflecting his background as an executive on a magazine known for its graphics, and his journalistic conservatism, Gart ordered a redesign of the *Star* that made the paper more attractive, but also a traditional vertical paper once again.

Some of the changes in the *Star* were good: its international coverage improved perceptibly and it ran many more stories than it had under Allbritton and Bellows. But the overall result was a *Star* that, while echoing an old-style paper in its design, actually was an old-style paper, full of short, mainly noninterpretative and mostly noninvestigative news stories—a paper that would have been read avidly by millions before television monopolized the purveying of hard, breaking news.

Gart's transformation of the *Star* might have worked had Time given him enough money to expand its news space and news staff to the size of the *Post*'s. Then many readers would have seen the *Star* as a real competitor to the *Post*, rather than as what amounted to a digest of it. But Time, Inc., although it more than fulfilled its pledge to spend $60 million on the *Star*, was fighting inflation, recession, and the *Post* all at once in D.C. The *Star* was kept on a tight budget.

Time did, though, make a move that would secure it the right to run Doonesbury and other comic strips and features in the *Star*. It spent an undisclosed amount of cash to acquire a minority interest in Universal Press Syndicate, which distributes Doonesbury and other features. In turn, Universal Press Syndicate took over the Washington Star Syndicate, which Time had acquired when it bought the *Star*.

The *Star*'s banner headlines and promotional stories about the comic strip it thus acquired, Doonesbury, so infuriated *Post* executive editor Ben Bradlee that he stopped running Doonesbury in the *Post* before the feature moved to the *Star*, saying he was not going to continue to promote a feature that would no longer be in the *Washington Post*.

Bradlee's action angered thousands of Washingtonians. Senators and congressmen denounced him. Radio and TV stations broadcast the missing Doonesbury sequences. The *Post*'s own ombudsman criticized Bradlee's conduct. The *Star*'s promo machine went into high gear, producing, among thousands of other items, bumper stickers reading "Follow Doonesbury to the *Star*!" Thousands of readers did, but they didn't stay for long.

Although he sometimes seemed to be taking the *Star* in the wrong direction, Gart did a number of good things for the paper. He improved the *Star*'s arts, books, and sports sections. He expanded the paper's op-ed page to three pages, in an attempt to add fresh viewpoints to the somewhat stale views of Washington's well-known columnists. He reinstituted a practice that had been abandoned by the *Star*: printing the full text of official speeches and documents so that the paper's readers could judge for themselves what the official involved had said. He ordered the energetic pursuit of the "Billygate" story in the pages of the *Star*. The paper's unbiased coverage of the 1980 presidential elections was a model of thorough journalism.

Gart argued that he was making the *Star* into the fully serious paper he felt it had to be to have standing in the community and to compete with the authoritative *Washington Post*.

His critics replied that the more the *Star* became like the *Post*, the less reason there was for anybody to buy the *Star*. Their argument was that the *Star* didn't have, never would have, the ability to match the gargantuan *Post* in the sheer volume of information that paper dumped on its subscribers' doorsteps every morning. The right tack, they believed, was the one Bellows and Allbritton had taken: pep up the *Star* so it danced rings around the ponderous *Post*.

Gart counterargued that the *Star* had continued to lose readers and advertisers under Allbritton and Bellows, so why should he perpetuate what they had been doing? He eliminated most of the features that, under Bellows and Allbritton, had made the *Star* so distinctive, although the "Ear" column was retained.

(Gart may have been right to eliminate the features. When he tried a pseudo-Bellows ploy on the front page, the ploy backfired. It was a new front-page feature called "Today's Violent Local Crime." A response to attacks on several *Star* staffers outside the *Star* building, located near an expressway in a deteriorating Washington neighborhood, the feature was, simply, a detailed description of the day's worst incident of criminal violence. It wasn't part of any larger anticrime crusade, and no one ever really explained what it was doing there. Many of the *Star*'s readers were disgusted by it. Gart said later that the feature was a "journalistic way of dramatizing something" and that it was meant "to heighten awareness that there were crimes being committed and that something ought to be done about them.")

Journalistic philosophy aside, Gart took a number of other steps that demoralized the *Star* staff and, at best, puzzled the paper's readers. One was running fawning stories about Time, Inc. in the pages of the *Star*.

For instance, when Time, Inc. introduced its new science magazine, *Discover*, the *Star* covered the debut with a pre-view article, a lengthy feature article, and, house-organ style, a lengthy story, complete with photos, on the magazine's christening party. Had a Time, Inc. public relations person even suggested that a newspaper two hundred fifty miles from the country's publishing capital give this much coverage to the introduction of a new magazine, he would have been hooted out the door.

Then when Andrew Heiskell, chairman of the board of Time, Inc., retired, the *Star* sent a reporter to New York to cover Heiskell's farewell party. The reporter's story ran, at length, accompanied by three flattering photos of Heiskell. Gart argued that by its purchase of the *Star*, Time, Inc. had become a major Washington employer and that some of the Time people profiled were major national figures in their own right or because of their positions at the top of the nation's largest publishing company. Gart, however, later admitted in an interview that there was too much of this sort of coverage in the *Star*, and that he was too wrapped up in Time, Inc. affairs.

Gart's preoccupation with Time, Inc. figures put the paper in embarrassing straits on occasion. In the summer of 1979, for instance, President Carter was about to nominate Thomas Watson, who headed IBM and sat on Time, Inc.'s Board of Directors, as ambassador to the Soviet Union. *Star* editorial writers rushed into print to blast Watson as a "businessman who does not speak Russian or have any special expertise in Soviet affairs." The editorial went on to say that some ambassadors "are expected to run embassies and negotiate with foreign governments; others sit behind the big desk under the Great Seal of the U.S. for different reasons." The editorial might have added that some ambassadorial nominees are not only appointed but editorially supported for "different reasons."

Gart said later that although he always read the *Star*'s editorials before they were printed, he had been out of town the day before the Watson editorial ran and hadn't seen it until he read it in the *Star*. After reading it, Gart said in an interview, he decided that it was "snide . . . and didn't describe the man I knew. I thought we should back up and do a piece on what the guy had done and then come back with a revised editorial expressing a much sounder view."

A story about Watson was duly written and printed in the paper's news columns. Unbylined and headlined "No Stranger to Russia," the story dealt with Watson's various trips to and experiences in Russia, including his ten-day vacation in that country after graduating from college and his having flown into Russia as a World War II Air Corps pilot.

A new editorial then appeared contending that Watson's nomination "is a reminder of how strong a case there is for not giving the post to a Foreign Service officer and for giving it to a knowing outsider such as Mr. Watson." Watson was nominated and confirmed as U.S. ambassador to the Soviet Union.

Gart argued later, "Do you act fairly toward someone who is in the same company you're in, or do you treat him unfairly because he's in the same company? In the end, you have to be fair."

The Watson stories, and others, reinforced the impression

that the paper had become a house organ for Time, Inc. Other newspapers have and will write puff pieces about their owners, but the *Star* wrote such stories in the pitiless glare of the floodlights trained not only on the world's news capital, but on the newest battle of the Washington titans, the *Washington Post* vs. the *Washington Star*.

Incredibly, after such displays of apparent favoritism, the *Star* launched a quarter-million-dollar, five-week television advertising campaign accusing the *Post* of bias. The first commercial in the campaign showed two newspapers enacting a Western-style shootout in a sea of fog. A voiceover called the newspaper on the left "slanted, one-sided, and biased" as the newspaper on the left began falling to the left. The remaining newspaper, unbloodied and unbowed, turned to face the audience and was revealed to be the *Star*. The ads were referring to what was said to be the *Post*'s liberal bias, but in view of what many felt was the *Star*'s new role—house organ for a giant New York corporation—the claim of relative superiority was laughable.

Gart was quite sincere and energetic, though, in his desire to resuscitate the *Star*. He made two major attempts to maneuver the paper out of the clutches of death in the afternoon.

Because the *Star*, by virtue of its afternoon delivery time, was competing with suburban newspapers throughout the area, Gart began four suburban editions of the paper, and one edition for D.C. He was particularly worried that a suburban chain of twice-weekly papers would begin publishing on a daily basis and attract more readers away from the *Star*. The *Star*'s zoned editions prevented that suburban chain from going daily, but they added further to the complexity of the paper's editorial and production problems.

Publishers often point out that, unlike other manufacturers, they put out a different product every day. Putting out six, seven, or eight different products every day, or at least every weekday, was much more difficult. For example, the same story would require the writing of twelve different headlines for its appearance under different guises in different editions. And the *Star* was unable to spend enough money on its suburban editions to solve the problems they caused.

Also adding immense complexity to the paper was the computer system Time purchased for it. The company made the mistake of purchasing the most advanced system available and unleashing it on the staff before the bugs were worked out of it, publisher Hoyt later admitted. Overloaded by the paper's numerous separate suburban editions, the system broke down regularly, several times a week and often on deadline. Tragically, it failed when it was most needed, hitting its low point by breaking down the day President Reagan was shot, leaving the *Star's* editors and reporters bug-eyed with frustration.

Gart also attempted to escape the afternoon trap altogether by beginning a morning edition. If he had had more money, he said, he would have moved the paper's main edition to the morning and put out only the paper's suburban editions in the afternoon, a unique solution that would have given the *Star* the best of both worlds. But to move the *Star's* main edition to the morning would have required setting up a morning home-delivery system, and this Time, Inc. refused to do.

It would have been expensive, of course, but James Shepley, Time, Inc. president and *Star* chairman, also argued that it would have been suicidal for the ailing *Star* to attempt a head-to-head confrontation with the morning, home-delivered *Washington Post*.

As it was, Time had tremendous problems getting the *Star* delivered at all. Some of the executives Time sent down to run the *Star* were inexperienced at the task of delivering a major metropolitan daily. To make things worse, those executives clashed among themselves, and with the unions involved.

Although much of its effort was misdirected, or self-destructive, or, partly for financial reasons, halfhearted, the *Star*, under both Allbritton and Time, helped prevent the *Washington Post* from dying of a severely swollen ego. A great many *Post* reporters had come to consider themselves celebrities. When successful, they wrote books, appeared on talk shows, and were invited to high-class parties. Even in failure, they were lionized. After the *Post* admitted that its Pulitzer Prize–winning story about an eight-year-old heroin addict, "Jimmy's World," was a phony, and returned the Pulitzer, *Post* ombudsman Bill Green wrote of "Jimmy's World" perpetrator Janet Cooke, a *Post* reporter, that "when she walked, she pranced. When she smiled, she dazzled." Would a reporter fired by the *Dayton Daily News* for turning in a phony story have been described this way? Green's description of Cooke was, in fact, embarrassingly similar to the *Star*'s descriptions of Time, Inc. bigwigs. But the *Star* had the right instincts when the *Post* faltered. The smaller paper jabbed its gargantuan opponent in the solar plexus on several occasions, most spectacularly by breaking the story that "Jimmy's World" was a hoax. Then, because a loser can't afford not to kick a winner when he's down, the *Star* ran its own series of stories on drug abuse among the young, accompanied by a box informing its readers that "the stories we tell here are true."

Aside from what it could do to the *Post*, the *Star* couldn't do much for itself. Though its circulation and ad linage rose after Gart began a morning edition, and during the first two years of Time, Inc. ownership, they began to fall off again. Moreover, while Shepley, through his national contacts, gained the *Star* an increased share of national advertising, the paper never made any headway with local advertisers.

If the paper could have regained 40 percent of the area's newspaper advertising, its executives thought, it might stay alive. To get advertising, though, it needed a sizable increase in circulation. But why should anyone read it? Suburban readers could read their suburban papers, and news junkies both inside and outside D.C. could gorge themselves on the *Post*.

The *Star*, filled mostly with short, straight stories and rewrites, had become the Six O'Clock News, minus the action and minus the color. You also had to buy it and get newsprint all over your hands rather than drink a beer in your easy chair while you watched the same news for free.

Near the end, as *Star* ad sales sagged perilously, the paper's ad salesmen were reduced to arguing that the *Star* was a better ad buy because advertisements placed in the *Star* would stand out dramatically in a paper half the size of the *Post* and carrying so small a percentage of the city's ad volume. This was equivalent to a one-legged man arguing that he should be hired to carry a heavy load because he wouldn't trip over his own feet the way two-legged laborers would.

On July 23, 1981, with the *Star*'s circulation at 300,000 (down from 349,000 the day Time bought it), its share of the Washington newspaper ad dollar at an all-time low, and its losses at $20 million a year, Time announced that the paper would publish its last issue August 7. (Time executives refused to admit that any of the changes they had made in the *Star* had anything to do with the paper's imminent demise. Time, Inc. editor-in-chief Henry Grunwald insisted that the

Star under Time was not only the best afternoon newspaper in the country but one of America's three or four best and most responsible newspapers, morning or evening. The *Star* was better than most American newspapers, but it wasn't that good.)

Although $20 million a year is a lot to lose, Time is big and rich, and had it been determined to win in Washington, it could have continued to run the *Star* while searching for ways to make it profitable once again. If the company had held on eighteen more months, for instance, the end of the recession would have given the *Star* a new chance at profitability. But whenever a big company does something it wants to do anyway, its executives argue that its shareholders wouldn't let it do otherwise. Time, Inc. is no exception. Its shareholders wouldn't have allowed the *Star* to continue operating in the face of such losses, Time executives later said.

More pertinent still, when the decision to close the *Star* was made, the major Time honchos who had decided to purchase the paper in the first place either had retired or were on the verge of doing so. Their successors, whose backgrounds were in business rather than journalism, were less interested in publishing per se. And, since the new Time, Inc. bosses hadn't made the original decision to purchase the *Star*, they felt much less responsibility to keep it open.

For six years before the fall, though, *Washington Post* management had expressed deep concern about the possibility of Washington becoming a one-newspaper town.

"We believe in a freely competitive press," the *Post* had thundered in a 1975 editorial, while Allbritton was maneuvering to buy the *Star*, "and that's precisely why we also believe the nation's capital needs at least two competing newspapers." When Time, Inc. bought the *Star*, *Post* chairman and president Katharine Graham announced, "We welcome Time, Inc. to the Washington newspaper field. We have the greatest respect for their publishing skills and feel sure the *Washington Star* will benefit greatly from its association with that company." When Gart arrived in town to take over the *Star*, *Post* executive editor Ben Bradlee wrote, "Welcome to our town. It's a good newspaper town, and it's going to be better because Murray's here." Bradlee also said, "No newspaper wants to be a monopoly."

Taking their cue from these inspiring statements and editorials, Time executives proposed to the *Post*, about four months before the *Star* closed, that the two papers join together under a joint operating agreement, a legally sanctioned arrangement under which the news and editorial operations of the two papers would have remained separate but their commercial functions would have been combined to cut operating costs and keep the *Star* going.

In return for the agreement, Time's executives offered to stop publishing the Saturday and Sunday editions of the *Star*, thus leaving the *Post* free of competition on the weekend. They also suggested that the *Star* switch entirely to the morning during the week as part of the arrangement. (It was projected that such a step would have reduced Time's losses on the paper from $20–$25 million to $5–$7 million annually, thus encouraging the company to keep the paper going much longer, and, not so incidentally, allowing it to escape death in the afternoon for good.)

The *Post*'s answer was delivered at the final negotiating session, held at Katharine Graham's house. Attending the session were Graham; her son, Donald Graham, who had succeeded her as publisher; and *Post* board member Warren Buffett. Mrs. Graham said that the *Post* would agree to a joint agency if Time would guarantee to the *Post*, as part of the joint operating agreement, the 13.5 to 15 percent profit margin the *Post* would make were it competing head to head with the ailing and lethargic *Star*. If the profits of the joint operation went above 15 percent, the two papers would divide the excess. If the profits fell below 13.5 percent, the *Star* would pay the *Post* the difference (but would be free to drop out of the joint operation one year after doing so).

Rather than commit themselves to an endless future as the *Washington Post*'s sugar daddies, *Time*'s executives ended the discussions. As a *Post* official put it, the larger paper had "prospects of profit margins" it didn't want to endanger.

Although they refused to call an ambulance for their dying friend, *Post* executives kept the sympathy notes coming. When the closing was formally announced, Mrs. Graham sent Gart a note of condolence handwritten on pale blue paper. "Dear Murray," the note began, "my heart is broken for you." Donald Graham wrote, "The demise of the *Star* is dreadful for Washington and for anyone who loves newspapers." Not dreadful enough to be worth risking the *Post*'s profit margins to avert, of course. Anyway, the *Post* would get most of the *Star*'s readers and advertisers as soon as the *Star* closed, so why bother?

Despite the *Post*'s lack of interest, sixteen potential buyers approached Time, Inc. about purchasing the *Star*. Some were representatives of special interests hoping to set up shop outside the White House gates; others were relatively benign.

Oil magnate Armand Hammer expressed an interest in the *Star*. So did conservative direct-mail expert Richard Viguerie; Mortimer Zuckerman, Boston real estate magnate and owner of *Atlantic Monthly*; and, most extraordinarily, Cris-Craft Industries, a New York–based conglomerate. (U.S. senators from Maryland and Virginia moved simultaneously but unsuccessfully to allow the company to take the *Star* as a tax writeoff.) Other offers came from groups in Tennessee and Chicago, and one came from a Canadian-based consortium that included the Dutch newspaper *De Telegraaf.*

Time insisted that any new buyer agree to spend $20 million and keep the *Star* going for at least a year after purchasing it. The company said its motive was to prevent someone from buying the *Star* at a low price, selling off the paper's physical assets, and leaving its fourteen hundred employees without the severance pay and pension benefits Time had promised them.

Despite these stringent requirements, a number of bids actually were made. But Time rejected bids offering less money than it wanted, and rejected other bids because the company wasn't convinced the bidders actually had the money they were offering. One bid was rejected because the bidder was a foreigner and another because the bidder was, in Time's view, an "unsuitable owner" of the *Star.* Time executives refused to identify either of these bidders but insisted that neither was Australian Rupert Murdoch.

Several bidders begged Time to keep the *Star* going for just a few more weeks while they negotiated with the *Star*'s traumatized unions for new concessions that would allow the paper to continue publishing. If Time had allowed them this short grace period, several investors insisted, they could have bought the paper and run it profitably.

Washington attorney Robert Linowes, whose brother, Sol M. Linowitz, was a member of the boards of both Time, Inc. and the *Star,* tried to interest local investors, and *Star* employees themselves, in purchasing the paper. The short period, however, between the announcement of closing and the closing date itself didn't leave him enough time either to organize the employee purchase or to complete the necessary renegotiation of union contracts.

Time refused to keep the *Star* open for more than two weeks after it announced the game was up. The company argued that announcing the *Star*'s closing had scared advertisers away from the paper and keeping the *Star* going a few extra weeks would cost much money.

Others pointed out that Time already had lost a lot of money on the paper and that if the company had been sincere in its desire to keep a second newspaper voice alive in the nation's capital, the giant publishing–television–forest-products combine wouldn't have begrudged the cash to run the paper for a few more weeks while someone else arranged to take it off Time's shoulders. After all, Time could have avoided such a squeeze by announcing that the *Star* was for sale without giving a closing date for the paper. The Tribune Co. did precisely that with the *New York Daily News* and that paper later more than regained the advertising it lost during the "For Sale" period.

But Time, Inc. gave many the impression that it would just as soon flee as quickly as possible from the scene of such corporate embarrassment. (While Time, Inc. waited out the two weeks before the announced closing date, Gart spent time on the phone trying to line up new jobs for the soon-to-be-unemployed *Star* staffers.) On August 7, 1981, the *Star* closed for good.

Adding insult to injury, the *Post* immediately began planning an afternoon newspaper of its own. The five-day-a-week paper would have been aimed at D.C. workers on their lunch hour, with a late afternoon edition aimed at homebound commuters. It would have been sold only on newsstands. Analysts said such a paper could make money if produced by a small staff. (The *Post* would have the capacity to print it because it had purchased the *Star*'s presses, trucks, and printing plant from Time, Inc. after the *Star* closed.) In 1972 the

Washington Daily News had sold 100,000 papers a day in D.C., from newsstands alone, in the single hour between noon and one o'clock. *Post* editors thought they could attract 150,000 readers daily with a mix of features, local news, and sports in the new paper.

The proposed publication, a tabloid everyone called Tab, might have worked by sidestepping the major bugaboo of afternoon papers: trying to force delivery trucks through rush-hour traffic.

But Tab's opponents argued that the *Post* staff might dislocate itself trying to produce both a morning and an afternoon paper, and the same energy might better be spent on the morning *Post*. Anyway, they argued, how much extra would advertisers be willing to pay for an ad in Tab if they already were paying for an ad in the widely read *Post*? Why think about newspapers when you can think about profits?

"The bottom line is that the *Post* afternoon edition won't be done unless it can make a profit quickly," one *Post* insider said.

Post executives soon dropped the idea, at least in part because the regular morning *Post* was being inundated by new readers. Its circulation went up much more rapidly than *Post* executives had anticipated, forcing the paper to scramble merely to get its morning edition out on time.

Ten thousand former *Star* readers became *Washington Post* subscribers within three weeks of the *Star*'s death. Within a short while, 50,000 more signed on.

Three months after the *Star* folded, the *Post* reported a 25 percent increase in daily circulation and a 16 percent increase in Sunday circulation. (By 1983 the *Post*'s daily circulation had risen to 748,000, and its Sunday circulation to a million.) The *Post*'s return on the $14 million it had spent on the *Star*'s presses and trucks was a newspaper with a circulation of

150,000—an $85 million value. The *Post* also loaded up on *Star* columnists and columns, including "Ear."

Very soon after plastering "Ear" on its head, however, the *Post* stuck its elbow in it. The column had made sense in the *Star*, which, being number two, wasn't taken as seriously as the *Post*. Readers had assumed the *Star* would make all sorts of noises to attract attention away from the grinding *Post* juggernaut, and "Ear" was assumed to make some of those noises.

President Carter, however, condemned the move to the *Post*, saying, "The decision by the publishers of a nationally and internationally influential newspaper like the *Post* to print a regular column which is widely known to be based on rumor and gossip adds unwarranted credence to its false reports."

What occasioned Carter's wrath was that "Ear" reported a rumor that Carter had bugged Blair House, the White House's guest house, when President-elect and Mrs. Reagan were staying there. It was pointed out that such a story, if true, deserved front-page headlines, not a paragraph in a gossip column in the "Style" section.

Like the politicians whom *Post* reporters have caught flagrante delicto in major indiscretions, the *Post* itself backed and then filled. First a *Post* editorial admitted that "Ear" had merely passed along a rumor the *Post* found "utterly impossible to believe." ("Ear" never actually said that the Carters had bugged the Reagans; it only reported what the hot new rumor was.) A number of *Post* reporters protested that the editorial made it sound as if unbelievable rumors were the basis of a large number of *Post* stories.

Finally, seeing the way things were going, *Post* publisher Donald Graham wrote a letter of apology to Carter. The letter backed away from the paper's original expression of disbelief in the story, called the source of the rumor credible, and insisted that although the *Post*'s editors had come to believe that the story was wrong, they had believed the story was true when it appeared in "Ear." The controversy died down, amid snickering, but the *Post* had been badly burned.

The brouhaha also deadened "Ear" awhile, until McLellan and her column migrated to the *Washington Times* (where her column was retitled "Diana Hears"). There McLellan could resume firing her witty darts at the *Post*, a practice that had been impossible when her column had been appearing in that paper.

But even with McLellan on the rampage once again, the *Post* looked a bit sickly without the *Star* to goad it. Some very small papers tried to pick up the ball Time, Inc. had dropped. One was the *Washington Tribune*, a free biweekly tabloid distributed in liquor stores and elsewhere within the District itself. The *Tribune* tried to cover the impact, on Washington's complex city neighborhoods, of the new Metro stops *Post* readers passed through on their way to and from the suburbs and the new shopping malls they strolled in during their lunch hours. The *Tribune* also published its own "inside gossip" column that tweaked the *Post* and fired zingers at its well-known staffers. The *Tribune*'s editor said the column's popularity indicated that D.C. readers were resentful of the journalistic dictatorship the *Post* had imposed on the District, with only the *Washington Times*, a paper backed by an offbeat religious group, to challenge its authority on a daily basis.

The *Times* and the *Tribune* aside, various suburban papers, competing with the *Post* for former *Star* readers, expanded their D.C. coverage to lure those readers. And the

New York Times added a page of Washington news and features to its daily paper. These offerings, however, paled to nothing when compared to the bright light of the old *Star.*

CHAPTER SIX

Oakland

There May Be a There There

The military administrator in the newly occupied Germany of 1945 could not take his eyes off the army newspaper he was reading.

The paper told him that California's United States senator, Hiram Johnson, had just died and that Gov. Earl Warren had appointed him, William Knowland, a thirty-seven-year-old army major, to take Johnson's place in the Senate.

Such news would have been gratifying to anyone at any time, but to Knowland in 1945 it was manna from heaven. His father, Joseph R. Knowland, had attempted to climb to the presidency but had made it only as far as the U.S. House of Representatives. Now he, Bill Knowland, was starting his political career at a higher level than his father had ended his. Bill Knowland couldn't wait to get going. Without bothering to change, he flew back to the States to be sworn in as a United States senator, still wearing his wrinkled khaki jacket and army trousers tucked into GI boots. He would be "the Knowland who would make it" to the top, to the White House.

Although immensely gratifying, the news wasn't totally unexpected. Bill Knowland was a born politician. He had begun his political career at age twelve by speaking in support of the Harding-Coolidge ticket. He had attended his first national convention at age sixteen. He had been elected a state assemblyman, then a state senator, and had been chosen as chairman of the Republican National Committee before joining the army in 1942.

He was supported in all this by something other than his political savvy and enthusiasm, something beyond his father's experience and political friends. Bill Knowland was supported by the *Oakland Tribune*, his father's newspaper. From the time Joe Knowland took over the paper in 1914, being supported by the *Oakland Tribune* meant a lot.

Gertrude Stein had said of Oakland, "There's no there there," but what did she know? Directly across San Francisco Bay from San Francisco itself, Oakland was "The City That Built San Francisco." San Francisco, with its rows of pastel shutters and clanging cable cars, its coffeehouses and its gay bars, was crowded delicately onto the end of the San Francisco peninsula and had nowhere to grow.

Brawny Oakland, which supported San Francisco with its blue-collar industrial muscle, sprawled heavily across the area known as the East Bay, shrouded by the smoke from its oil refineries, shipyards, and lumber mills. And it supported the *Oakland Tribune*. With a circulation of 226,000, the *Tribune* was the largest afternoon newspaper in Northern California. It also was, far and away, the dominant newspaper in the East Bay and one of the state's political powerhouses. Under Joe Knowland the paper, as conservative in its news columns as on its editorial page, made and unmade California politicians, and few Republicans even thought of running for office without the paper's backing.

This mattered little to Major, now Senator, Bill Knowland. Certainly the paper's dominant political position had encouraged the Republican governor Warren to appoint him to the U.S. Senate. Moreover, with his father as owner, the paper could hardly fail to support him when he ran for reelection, or—for higher office. Bill Knowland, however, was going to make it to the top on his own. The Roosevelt era obviously was coming to an end. Soon it would be the Republicans' turn to rule once again, and Bill Knowland would ride the Republican wave right into the White House.

Knowland soon found an outlet for his conservatism: supporting the Nationalist Chinese government on Formosa. He became one of Chiang Kai-shek's strongest supporters and a bitter foe of allowing the communist regime in Peking a seat in the United Nations. So strong were his beliefs on this subject, and so voluble was he in his support of Nationalist China—which, after all, shared the Pacific Rim with California—that he became known as the senator from Formosa.

In the era of the Korean War and of anticommunist witch hunts in the U.S., Knowland's China stand was a popular one. He rose quickly from the status of youngest U.S. senator to become one of the most prominent members of that august body. In 1952 both major candidates for the Republican presidential nomination—Gen. Dwight D. Eisenhower and the Ohio senator Robert A. Taft—seriously considered Knowland for the Republican vice presidential nod.

But another man was chosen instead: Richard Nixon, who, as a member of the House Committee on Un-American Activities, had revealed the alleged treachery of State Department official Alger Hiss to a shocked America. Bill Knowland, however, was not a man to sulk or to seek revenge. Later, when Nixon went from the vice presidency to the presidency and, as president, embraced the China that Knowland had hated with a deep and a patriotic hatred,

Knowland neither denounced him nor opposed his 1972 reelection bid.

Though he had failed to obtain the vice presidential nomination in 1952, Knowland kept fighting. For a short while, the sun continued to shine on him. In 1954 Taft, the Senate majority leader, died and Knowland was elected majority leader in his place. He had reached his peak as U.S. senator. It also was the peak of his success.

The rest of his life would be plagued with a series of bad decisions that would have a devastating effect on him and on the *Oakland Tribune*. From 1954 on, Bill Knowland and his family were on the wrong side more often than not: the wrong side in local politics, the wrong side of local racial tensions, the wrong side of the flight to the suburbs, the wrong side of the bay, and the wrong side in the newspaper wars.

At the time, though, all that Knowland could see was that he now held the top Senate post. All he needed to do, he thought, was to get some experience as a chief executive of the state and then make a run at the White House.

In 1958 he returned to California to run for governor, although Goodwin J. Knight, a fellow Republican, sat in the governor's ramshackle mansion in Sacramento and wanted to stay there. The California Republican party squared off into Knight and Knowland factions and a huge intraparty brawl erupted. Republican leaders managed to settle the conflict by convincing Knight to let Knowland run for governor while Knight ran for the U.S. Senate.

The agreement, known derisively as the Big Switch, ended the intraparty feud but stank in the public nostrils. Californians who had perceived Knowland as a conservative of integrity now saw him as a grasping opportunist. And his conservatism didn't go down too well in California when applied to state issues. Part of his campaign for governor consisted of energetic support of a right-to-work initiative widely perceived as a union-busting measure. Attorney General Edmund G. (Pat) Brown, the Democratic candidate, overwhelmed Knowland at the polls.

It was Knowland's first political defeat. It was also his last. With the liberal tidal wave of the 1960s approaching, Knowland was through as a politician and knew it. He never ran for political office again.

He was a man of tremendous energy, however. That energy had to have an outlet and the outlet was Oakland and the *Tribune*. He became *Tribune* publisher and dedicated the rest of his life to using the *Tribune* as a hammer to build Oakland: build its Coliseum complex, build its museums complex, build its rapid-transit system. He continued to participate in politics, but as a publisher, not as a candidate.

Moreover, in keeping with the developing ethics of journalism, Knowland restricted the *Tribune's* political king-making to the paper's editorial columns, although he must have been tempted to slant the paper's political coverage in 1964, when he was the Northern California chairman of Barry Goldwater's bid for the presidency, and in 1966, when Knowland's nemesis, Gov. Pat Brown, was challenged by gubernatorial candidate Ronald Reagan.

Neutralizing the *Tribune's* news columns was undoubtedly the right thing to do. Few American newspapers lasted into the 1980s with their news columns full of unabashed political partisanship. But Knowland was a politician, not a newspaperman, as was his second-in-command at the *Tribune*, his former Senate aide, Paul G. Manolis, and in 1967 he offset the neutralizing of the *Tribune's* news columns with a tragic mistake.

A year after his father died and he became editor and

president of the *Tribune* as well as its publisher, Bill Knowland severely slashed the *Tribune's* suburban coverage and decided to concentrate on making it a city newspaper. In an area then dominated by clogged freeways, suburban sprawl, inadequate public transit, a battery of TV stations, and a powerful areawide morning newspaper—the *San Francisco Chronicle*—this move was the equivalent of praying to be afflicted with afternoon newspaper disease.

The *Tribune* had been the white middle-class East Bay newspaper, with a series of well-staffed suburban bureaus throughout the area, a paper as much at home in suburban backyards as the sound of children's laughter or the whir of powermowers. As a result of Knowland's fateful decision, however, the paper was forced to concentrate its appeal on the aging residents of Oakland proper. The older white people in Oakland still read it religiously but could hardly be counted on to ensure the paper's future.

Meanwhile, Oakland had become a black city. Oakland's blacks, correctly perceiving the *Tribune* as a paper run by a white Republican family untouched by the needs or concerns of blacks, didn't read it.

As middle-class whites left for the suburbs, which only the suburban papers made an effort to cover, the *Tribune's* circulation dropped from a 1968 peak of 226,000 to 187,000 in 1974. Meanwhile, the *San Francisco Chronicle*, with its mixture of popular columnists, heavy concentration on the bizarre and the sexy, and almost total belief in news as entertainment, surged forward in the circulation wars.

Perhaps Knowland's concentration on center-city projects blinded him to the idiocy of cutting suburban coverage in an era of tremendous suburban growth. Perhaps, by cutting suburban expenditures, he was merely yielding to his politically conservative passion for balanced budgets. (In this sense, at least, his policy worked; under the Knowlands the *Tribune* made money, although a steadily declining amount of money, every year.)

In line with this budget-cutting philosophy, very little replaced the suburban coverage that had been cut. Wire copy was used to cover national and international news. Local reporters covered politics, the courts, and the police (almost always from the police point of view), wrote cute features, and reported on manufactured events PR people dreamed up for their clients.

Oakland was the home of Huey Newton and the Black Panthers. San Francisco was just across the bay, tumultuous Berkeley was just to the north, and the dynamic West Coast all around Oakland was bubbling and changing, but the excitement the area produced wasn't reflected in the *Tribune*'s news coverage.

Two university studies of the *Tribune* under Knowland summed up the paper. Its political coverage was described as "totally objective," a vast improvement over the old *Tribune*, but its general coverage was described as "turgid," a decided failure in the face of what it could be.

Although Knowland succeeded in balancing the *Tribune*'s budget year after year, he failed at balancing his own. Working to build Oakland wasn't as exciting to him as maneuvering for power at the zenith of American politics. So he started spending time in Las Vegas, seeking that spine-tingling rush that comes from dropping thousands of dollars onto green felt and stepping off into the unknown. In addition, his personal life was in shambles. After a few flings in glittering Vegas, Knowland, by then sixty-three, had divorced the wife he had married some forty years before and had married a much younger woman he had met in the gambling capital. A short while later, after a few more flings, he found himself

$900,000 in debt. He began having trouble with his new wife. And he couldn't have failed to perceive that the newspaper he had inherited from his father was, in the words of one critic, "sailing gracefully into the mud."

In February 1974, two days after the declining *Tribune* celebrated its hundredth anniversary, and just two years after his second marriage, William Fife Knowland drove to his summer home north of San Francisco and fired a bullet into his brain.

In the wake of this tragedy a bizarre, creative, and contradictory figure appeared: Bill Knowland's son Joseph W. Knowland, who became *Tribune* publisher under the terms of his father's will. He immediately appointed himself editor as well—"Wouldn't you?" he asked—and for good measure gave his mother the job of book editor.

Joe Knowland was an actor, a man of the theater. He loved to do pratfalls and spoke a mile a minute in a high-pitched voice. When more conservative men would say "et cetera, et cetera," Joe Knowland would say "zappa zappa zappa."

On being interviewed by the solemn *Los Angeles Times* after he took over the *Tribune*'s top post, Knowland started to refer to the speed at which he thought the *Tribune* should improve. Suddenly, he broke into song. "We're late, we're late, for a very important date," he sang. "No time to say hello-goodbye, we're late we're late we're late."

A master of the theatrical gesture, Knowland tried to make the *Tribune* more exciting by giving it some of his personality. He "shazammed" his way from department to department, talking, laughing, joking, and trying to shake up a depressed and lethargic staff. As he did so, the mostly white-shirted, wingtip-wearing white male reporters and editors looked at him and shook their heads. Knowland had worked in journalism and at the *Tribune* all his life, though, and he applied his knowledge of the theater and his "zappa zappa zappa" personality to changing the paper as well as amusing himself.

He tried to loosen things up in the stolid, self-involved *Tribune* newsroom by suggesting that everyone come to work in a T-shirt or a funny hat. He called meetings for 10:04 A.M. instead of 10:00 A.M. to indicate precisely when the meetings would start. When he decided to raise the street-sale price of the *Tribune*, he invited all his editors into his office and had them empty their pockets or purses of change. He then had them dive into the pile of coins. After much jingling and jangling and many coins rolling off into corners had occurred, the quarter was found to be the most common coin present. Knowland immediately announced that he would raise the price of the *Tribune* to twenty-five cents. (Before he did, though, he had surveys taken to make sure the quarter actually was the most common coin people carried. Since it was, and most of the *Tribunes* that weren't home-delivered were sold in coin-operated racks, the increase to twenty-five cents—rather than, say, twenty cents—was a good move.)

The paper, stolid and old-fashioned looking, was redesigned. Racy pictures and cash contests appeared on the front page. Stories became shorter. Guest editorials appeared on the editorial page. A "Rap-Up" section aimed at young people lightened the paper considerably until Knowland thought better of it. When a guy walked in off the street and said he could duplicate one of Houdini's famous escape stunts in less time than Houdini took, Knowland hung the chap upside down in a straitjacket outside the *Tribune*'s twelfth-story window. When the escape artist beat Houdini's record, as promised, Knowland reported the story on the *Tribune*'s front page. The paper became lighter and less serious as a result of all this, and much more attractive.

A man who sang songs from "Alice in Wonderland" in his publisher's office atop the Tribune Tower, and who shook up the news sections of the *Tribune* as much as young Knowland had, was not going to accept outdated shibboleths about the *Tribune*'s editorial pages either.

In the interest of journalistic objectivity, he backed away from using the *Tribune* as a bludgeon to compel the building of major civic projects, and lessened his own involvement in community-chest-type groups. He allowed the *Tribune* to begin endorsing Democrats as well as Republicans on its editorial pages.

When told that all the newspapers in the area, including the *Tribune*, had been printing press releases from the Symbionese Liberation Army verbatim, because the SLA had threatened to kill the kidnapped Patty Hearst if its releases were altered, Knowland ran a front-page editorial denouncing this knuckling under and reminding his fellow editors of the responsibilities of the press under the First Amendment. Everybody began covering the SLA normally once again, using only edited portions of the outlawed army's press releases.

When Knowland realized that a pollution series run by the *Tribune* a couple of years before had resulted in absolutely no change in polluting practices, he threatened in an editorial to sue the antipollution authorities for failing to enforce the antipollution laws and got things moving once again.

Knowland could be faulted for adding too much spice and not enough substance to the paper, but someone had to shake it up. As Knowland shoved new features into the paper, he revived its moribund suburban coverage and even attempted to begin covering that part of Oakland the *Tribune* traditionally had ignored: the black part. His white editors were recalcitrant, however, and the black people of Oakland refused to believe that this young man who had inherited a traditionally white-oriented newspaper really meant it when he said he wanted to change it.

As Knowland questioned old assumptions and tried one method after another to pry the paper out of the mud, he turned off a number of his staffers but turned on the community. *Tribune* circulation began to climb back up. From a low of 166,000 in 1975, it rose to 175,000 in 1976, a long way from the paper's peak of 226,000 but a significant climb above the depths to which it had fallen.

Had circulation continued to improve and had Knowland had time to sort out his ideas, expand suburban coverage, and convince Oakland's black people he really meant to cover them, his staffers might have begun to overlook his theatrics, or to accustom themselves to his antics, and done more to help him improve the *Tribune*. But Knowland had to use the profits the *Tribune* was producing to pay for his innovations, rather than distribute them to the stockholders. Knowland says he told the stockholders, all Knowland family members, that as its circulation rose, the paper would attract more ads and produce more money to pay out to the stockholders, but a majority of the stockholders, led by Joe's cousin Jay Knowland, didn't like the way things were going.

Jay, who had worked in various businesses, couldn't help noticing that although he had millions of dollars' worth of stock in the Oakland Tribune Company, he was perpetually broke, whereas Joe, who held very little stock, was earning $95,000 a year as publisher.

When Jay asked Joe for a post at the paper he was given a trainee job at a low salary instead of the executive post he had expected. Joe, who had worked his way up through the *Tribune* ranks, wanted Jay to do the same, but Jay just couldn't keep his mind off the difference between Joe's income and his. He didn't think Joe was doing a good job with the paper and believed that the family's talent for running newspapers had died with Bill Knowland.

After months of bitter musing, he decided what to do. It took a bit of maneuvering, but after some effort he got a majority of the stockholders behind him and started looking around for someone to buy the *Tribune*. Joe and his allies took the issue to court but, with only a minority of the stockholders behind them, all they could do was move the actual conduct of the sale from Jay's hands into their own.

In the small school of potential afternoon newspaper buyers, only a few fish were big enough to swallow even a moderate-sized paper like the *Tribune*. Some of the biggest— Gannett Company for one—rejected the flirtatious overtures from the *Tribune* majority. Capital Cities Communications also was approached, but a Capital Cities executive, after a tour of the paper, described the *Tribune* building as an "armpit" and his company decided it wasn't in the deodorant business. Other firms entered into serious negotiations with the *Tribune* stockholders. Inevitably, some of the same big barracuda who had pursued the ailing *Washington Star* and *Philadelphia Bulletin* swam over to nibble at the stricken *Tribune*.

John McGoff, who allegedly had tried to buy the *Star* with South African money, made a serious offer. But the *Tribune* stockholders could imagine the ruckus a supporter of the racist South African government might stir up in a city with a black majority and rejected his bid.

The parade of serious and not so serious buyers, though, inspired Joe Knowland to one last flight of theatrical fancy. He still occupied himself after hours as an actor, and one night he found himself dressed for a performance as a professor of music at Leipzig University, and thoroughly disguised by his costume. He knew the *Tribune* city-room staffers were tense and nervous at the prospect of the paper's sale to unknown masters or, worse yet, its closing.

So Knowland decided to relieve their tension by visiting the city room in the guise of a German businessman interested in buying the place. Putting on a thick Teutonic accent to go with his costume, he strode around the city room announcing in stentorian tones what horrible things he planned to do with everyone present once he owned the paper. Finally, in a mock-Hitlerian monologue, he denounced "dat crazy publisher" for not agreeing to sell him the paper immediately. Work came to a complete halt in the newsroom as Knowland von Knowland ranted and raved. His tirade finally came to an end when the paper's security guards, by prearrangement with Knowland, rushed in to drag him away. He then revealed his true identity, to the applause of the staff.

The skit might have seemed less funny had many among Knowland's audience known what their fate under the real buyer was going to be. He was none other than Karl Eller (who, later, in partnership with Charter Co., would buy the *Philadelphia Bulletin*). In May 1977 Eller's Combined Communications Company bought the *Tribune* for $18 million in cash and real estate.

Although the new owners immediately fired Joe Knowland (Joe, though deprived of the *Tribune* as his stage, continued with his acting career), they seemed to pick up something of his theatrical approach toward managing and promoting the *Tribune*. Eller announced his purchase of the paper with a multimedia show at a downtown theater featuring jazzy slides of the paper, the region, and CCC's other operations, and highlighted by upbeat music.

The show was great entertainment, but from some points

of view, the other CCC operations it highlighted might better have been left in the dark. CCC owned seven television stations, six radio stations, and ten billboard companies, but only one other newspaper, the *Cincinnati Enquirer*, which it had acquired in 1975. One thing that separates TV and radio stations and billboard companies from newspapers is that the former have few employees whereas the latter are crawling with them. So along with redesigning the paper and launching a drive for new subscriptions, CCC put a lot of emphasis on getting rid of many of the *Tribune*'s employees.

Hard-line editors were hired, men who, according to the reporters involved, had no compunctions about playing Knowland's German role for tears rather than laughs. Reporters considered expendable were called up to the city desk and denounced for incompetence and stupidity while their colleagues cringed. Within a short while, thirty-five editorial staffers decided that keeping a job on a dying afternoon newspaper wasn't worth such humiliation, and quit.

One of the editors who pressured many staffers to leave referred in an interview to the reporters he was trying to get rid of as "right-wing hacks . . . people who couldn't write . . . the kind of people who do rough drafts of their stories" (a no-no among professional journalists). Several of the editors CCC hired believed the company was pushing these people out not only for the good of the paper but so that CCC could milk the *Tribune* for whatever profit the old girl could produce before CCC inevitably sold her. "We just wanted to make money on it," the new owner, Eller, said years later.

Although the forced resignations did keep the *Tribune* profitable—it made $2 million during the final year of CCC ownership—the staff reduction meant cuts in coverage, and the paper's circulation dropped from the peak of 175,000 that Joe Knowland had achieved to 168,000, close to where it had been when Knowland first took over.

Eller realized that one of the *Tribune*'s problems was that it was published in the afternoon. So he started a morning edition of the paper as a tentative step toward moving the whole operation to the A.M. within two years. The *Tribune*'s "Sunrise Edition," though, was no better than the afternoon *Tribune*.

Yet even as staffers and subscribers fled the paper in panic, the hoofbeats of rescue could be heard from afar.

The rescuer was a highly surprising one: the Gannett Company, a media chain which previously had rejected the idea of purchasing the *Tribune*. Gannett had established itself as a solid profiteer by buying money machines: monopoly newspapers in medium-sized cities where neither advertisers nor readers had anywhere else to go. By 1979 the company owned seventy-nine newspapers, making it the country's largest newspaper chain as well as its most profitable.

Still, Gannett had not even begun to satisfy its hunger for huge gobs of revenue. The really spectacular profits were in radio and television stations, and the company owned only one of each. The voracious Gannetters, still chewing on their accumulated newspaper morsels, looked hungrily at CCC's seven television stations and thirteen radio stations, most of them pulling down huge profits in large cities. In 1979 Gannett pounced, merging with CCC and acquiring everything that company owned for $370 million.

Almost as an afterthought, Gannett executives realized that along with CCC's broadcast stations and billboard companies, they had purchased not only the *Cincinnati Enquirer* but the *Oakland Tribune* as well.

It would be hard to think of a more unlikely Gannett newspaper than the *Tribune*: a declining newspaper in a major black industrial city facing stiff competition from a raft of suburban papers and from two area giants, the *San Francisco Chronicle* and *Examiner*. Many Gannett newspapers are relatively uninspiring "profit centers," but the chain realized that the *Tribune* needed quality therapy and needed it fast if it were to survive at all, much less become a contributor to Gannett's swelling coffers. Besides, it's hard to believe there wasn't some corporate ego involved, or that Gannett wasn't interested in showing the world how well it could do in a big-city situation in which it didn't hold all the marbles from the beginning. Their overriding concern, however, Gannett executives said, was to retain the paper, in Gannett lingo, as a "viable franchise," to do something with it that would eventually turn it into a profit center.

Credit Gannett for trying the most radical therapy available: it appointed a black man to run the *Tribune*. To the uninitiated, a black person might seem the logical editor for a paper in a town that had become 60 percent black. "Better than some wonderful white fellow from a Mississippi plantation," one Gannett executive quipped. Yet there are plenty of other black cities in the U.S. and not one of them had a black person running a major metropolitan daily until Gannett appointed Robert Maynard as *Tribune* editor-in-chief in September 1979. When the lords of the press lecture their fellow citizens on the need to end discrimination in this country, they might want to reflect on how long it took them to allow a black person to reach the position Maynard achieved. Even thirty years after the modern civil rights movement began, 20 percent of Americans are members of minority groups but only 5.6 percent of reporters or editors on daily newspapers are.

When Maynard, after years of writing for black newspapers, tried to break into the daily white press, he sent out more than three hundred letters and résumés, only to be rejected with excuses such as, "We've already got our Negro" or "My staff wouldn't accept it." When he finally got a job on a white daily newspaper—the York (Pa.) *Gazette and Daily*—in 1961, and was shown his typewriter, he was so overwrought with excitement that he promptly got his first nosebleed since childhood. He worked in York for six years before going to Harvard as a Nieman Fellow, then went to the *Washington Post* as a reporter and became ombudsman and editorial writer there. He then moved to Berkeley, just north of Oakland, to direct a program sponsored by Gannett and others aimed at training minorities for jobs in journalism, before taking over the editor's job at the *Tribune.*

What made Maynard's appointment so important to the *Tribune*'s news coverage was that under the Knowlands and CCC, the paper had to some extent ignored blacks unless they were arrested. Before Maynard, it was quite possible for a black resident of Oakland to live, play, work, serve, contribute, build, grow old, and die in the city without once appearing in the pages of its only daily newspaper unless he was arrested for robbing a liquor store. Maynard changed all that. Soon blacks began appearing on the *Tribune*'s feature pages for the same reasons whites appeared there; because they grew cabbages that looked like Winston Churchill, because they had interesting jobs, because everyone in the family had cancer, or for some other legitimately newsworthy angle that had nothing to do with race. The *Oakland Tribune* discovered that interesting characters could be black as well as white.

Maynard also tried to reduce the use of photographs of blacks caught in criminal acts. He once severely dressed down a subeditor for running on the *Tribune*'s front page a picture of little photographic worth of an obviously demented black man, grinning insanely and holding a knife after stabbing and killing another man. He was being subdued by spray from high-powered firehoses at a construction site in Philadelphia. Why this picture had been run on the front page of the *Oakland Tribune*, a continent away, was a puzzle.

Maynard encouraged the use of photos of blacks as normal people. He ordered coverage of community events never covered before, such as black sports tournaments, and of diseases rarely covered before, such as sickle-cell anemia. Maynard also improved the *Tribune* in general, by hiring many more reporters, including women and minorities, and by running long takeouts on community problems such as drugs, jobs, the schools, and the high local murder rate.

He also tried to close the gap between the newspaper and the community by spending much time at meetings of community organizations, both white and black, and devoting a regular chunk of the *Tribune*'s editorial page to a "Letter from the Editor," an attempt to communicate to the readers what was going on at the *Tribune* and to discuss community concerns shared by blacks and whites.

The *Tribune* improved greatly under Maynard's stewardship, but both Maynard and Gannett knew that improving the paper, and bringing racial justice to its pages and its city room, might bring the paper greater community respect, and maybe even increased circulation, but it would not make it profitable. This was partly because Oakland, unlike, say, Washington and Philadelphia, had taken the final step in ghettoization: most of the major stores, the paper's major advertisers, had followed the whites to the suburbs. No matter how good the *Tribune* became, if it was read by Oakland residents only, it would continue to slide down the demand curve into advertising oblivion.

The paper had to appeal to suburbanites and, as afternoon

newspaper disease had shown everywhere in America, its best chance was in appealing to them in the morning, long before they could read about their home communities in their local suburban newspapers. But the area already had a major morning newspaper, the *San Francisco Chronicle*. If the *Tribune* simply moved to the morning, it would lose many of its hard-core afternoon readers and wrench precious few ads and steady customers away from the dominant *Chronicle*.

The only thing to do was start a new morning newspaper to attract a new audience and new advertisers while keeping the old audience and advertisers by revitalizing the afternoon *Tribune*. Then, with both an a.m. and a p.m. paper in operation, the company could look at the ad and circulation figures for each and decide whether to stay in the afternoon or migrate to the morning.

For a company that already had produced *Cocoa Today* in Florida, *Westchester Today* in New York, and was soon to produce *USA Today* all over America, only one name seemed feasible for its new creation: *Eastbay Today*.

Eastbay Today came out in time for the morning rush hour and featured shorter stories, and stories with more areawide appeal, than its afternoon counterpart. It also carried peach-colored sports and business sections advertised by the slogan, "Reach for the Peach." Gannett spent millions on printing, promoting, and selling *Eastbay Today*, and holding the price down to ten cents a copy. (The company tried to save money where it could, by using *Tribune* staffers as *Eastbay Today* staffers, and, of course, by using the *Tribune* presses to print the new paper.)

The company's gamble paid off, at least in popularity. The afternoon *Tribune* lost some readers, but the spunky new *Eastbay Today* attracted many more, and by September 1979 the total circulation of both *Eastbay Today* and the *Tribune* had hit 220,000, only 6,000 below the *Tribune*'s all-time circulation peak. Advertising in both papers also increased as Gannett offered advertisers a free ad in *Eastbay Today* for every ad put in the *Tribune*.

Eastbay Today was so successful, in fact, that in 1982 Maynard and Gannett decided to move the *Tribune* to the morning, merge it with *Eastbay Today*, and attempt to attract everyone in the community to the favored morning time slot. (*Eastbay Today*'s circulation was growing, and readership surveys had shown that most of the *Tribune*'s afternoon readers would switch to the morning if some of the features running in the afternoon *Tribune* were transferred to the morning paper.)

But while Maynard was looking longingly at the morning, Gannett was looking longingly at television once again.

Gannett had shown what it could do—produce a high-minded, serious, racially just newspaper in the afternoon, and a jaunty version of the same paper in the morning, and attract the readers and advertisers who might eventually make the whole operation profitable. No longer would Gannett executives have to hang their heads at newspaper conventions when executives of embattled big-city newspapers talked about their struggles. After Oakland, Gannett had been there too, and had emerged with flags flying and heads high (although, after making money on the paper during its first year of ownership, Gannett had lost a total of about $2 million on the *Tribune* and *Eastbay Today*, its executives say).

Having shown how well it could perform under fire, however, the company suddenly realized that while it was spending millions improving the *Tribune* and marketing *Eastbay Today*, the largest TV station in romantic San Francisco was seductively waving thousand-dollar bills in its direction and winking provocatively.

One week after Maynard announced he would move the *Tribune* to the morning and merge it with *Eastbay Today*, just when the whole operation was turning the corner, Gannett announced it would swap $100 million and its Oklahoma City TV station for the *San Francisco Chronicle*'s San Francisco TV station, KRON—and sell both the *Tribune* and *Eastbay Today*.

Gannett pointed out that Federal Communications Commission rules prohibited the same company from owning both a newspaper and a broadcast outlet in the same market.

Observers noted, though, that only lucre's lure forced Gannett to buy KRON at all and that, while putting the *Tribune* on the block, the company made it very clear it intended to hold on for dear life to the *San Rafael Independent Journal*, another newspaper it owned in the same area. The San Rafael paper, blanketing rich, white, and suburban Marin County, was one of the papers whose presses Gannett was using to help print the national Gannett newspaper, *USA Today*.

(Gannett argued that the FCC rules that applied to the *Tribune* wouldn't be applied to the *Journal* because the *Journal* was so much smaller than the *Tribune*. Whereas ownership of KRON and the *Journal* could not be conceived of as dominating the area, owning KRON and the *Tribune* could be, Gannett executives said. Several area newspaper publishers disagreed and made plans to fight Gannett's continued ownership of the San Rafael paper.)

Maynard insisted he didn't feel deserted by Gannett. "It's their right to look for a way to make more money," he said. "That's the business they're in."

He immediately set about finding a way to maintain control of the paper himself. Nine months later, in April 1983, he found a way. He purchased the paper himself, and became editor, publisher, and president of the new company. Gannett gave Maynard the help he needed to take this step. The company lowered its asking price for the *Tribune*, loaned Maynard a large portion of the purchase price on easy repayment terms, ate the losses the paper had suffered during the *Eastbay Today* years—and left the *Tribune* a massive legacy of trucks, presses, and newspaper racks.

Maynard also was assisted by the *Tribune*'s unions. In what is becoming standard practice in afternoon newspaper country, Maynard convinced the unions to agree to various labor and wage concessions—moderate, in this case—which, it was predicted, would save the *Tribune* $10 million over the next five years.

In return, Maynard promised the unions what every employer in a similar situation has been promising in recent years, a portion of the profits. In the *Tribune*'s case, Maynard promised the paper's employees 20 percent of the *Tribune*'s after-tax profits above $2.5 million annually. He then appointed seven outside directors to advise the new company, including former U.S. ambassador to Ghana Shirley Temple Black and *Roots* author Alex Haley.

Maynard himself boldly predicted new profits and said he and the *Tribune* wanted to make it on their own, without the subsidies Gannett had been providing. "I didn't come here to create the only newspaper in America that lived off welfare," he quipped.

Meanwhile, Gannett's rationale for selling the *Tribune* evaporated. The owners of KRON-TV originally wanted to sell their station because they were pessimistic about the station's future, and, in the long run, about the future of NBC, the station's parent network.

Gannett's official purchase of the station, however, was delayed for a year by various unrelated matters, and during that period, KRON's owners began to wonder what they were doing. The station's ratings, and NBC's ratings, began a gradual upswing, and steps were taken to revitalize the station itself. In the minds of its owners, KRON's profit potential rose.

Meanwhile, the Oklahoma City station Gannett wanted to trade for KRON was running into stiffening competition and that station's network, ABC, was having troubles of its own. Furthermore, the Oklahoma City market, hard hit by the drop in oil and gas prices, was showing weaknesses. Finally, KRON's owners decided they didn't want to sell at all, leaving Gannett standing nearly empty-handed in the Bay Area with neither the *Tribune* nor the station.

The *Tribune* itself was once again in rough waters. When it merged with *Eastbay Today* it lost some of its hard-core afternoon readers, and when, out of necessity, it raised the price of the new morning paper to twenty-five cents (the price of the old afternoon *Tribune*) it lost more readers, and its circulation dropped back to 167,000 in 1983.

As a newly minted morning paper, the *Tribune* had to begin competing directly with the *San Francisco Chronicle* for readers and advertisers. It also had to appeal across the board to the entire community. When it was Oakland's white paper, it didn't have to worry about alienating Oakland's blacks. Now it had to worry about blacks and whites (and orientals and Hispanics) in both city and suburbs if it was to survive.

But how long would whites buy a paper that, by attempting to portray Oakland accurately, might seem unduly concerned with blacks? And how long would Oakland's blacks continue to buy a paper that might seem unduly concerned with the area's suburban whites?

The problem was worse in Oakland than in many other cities because of the existence of an attractive alternative, the *San Francisco Chronicle* and *Examiner*, operating cheaply as a joint operation under the protection of the federal Newspaper Preservation Act. The *Chronicle*, although it covered the whole area, rarely seemed to cover anything seriously, and thus alienated few readers, and the *Examiner* was so much the junior partner of the *Chronicle* that it had little effect on reader perceptions.

Today Maynard makes endless appearances in the community, setting up *Tribune* citizen advisory groups in every part of the area, and continues his efforts in his "Letter from the Editor" columns, as well as through story selection and the improvement of the *Tribune*, to bridge the gap between blacks and whites. He persists both for the sake of media justice and in hopes of keeping the *Tribune* alive as a serious areawide newspaper.

Can Maynard keep the *Tribune* going long enough to allow him to solve one of America's major domestic problems, its racial gap? Gannett gave him a good start, and Maynard sidestepped afternoon newspaper disease by moving to the morning, but he and his local backers have nowhere near the money Gannett had with which to refloat the *Tribune* if it should again run onto a financial shoal. Soon Maynard might feel compelled to compete with the *Chronicle* by offering froth and entertainment as news, and white faces instead of black ones to placate advertisers and suburbanites.

If he sticks rigidly to his guns, and a significant number of readers and advertisers buy the *Chronicle* instead of the *Tribune*, Maynard and his new morning newspaper may vanish from the scene, leaving Oakland as the largest city in America without its own daily newspaper.

If he can continue to cover both city and suburbs and

address the needs and capture the interest of both blacks and whites in the East Bay, he may save the *Tribune*.

CHAPTER SEVEN

Down and Dirty

The *Her-Ex* Takes a Nosedive

William Randolph Hearst, publisher of the *San Francisco Examiner*, rode out of the West in 1895 with guns blazing and set the newspaper world on fire. Hearst had a formula. He titillated his readers with lurid and sensational coverage of crime, sex, and scandal, mostly among the upper classes, and devoted the remaining space in his newspaper to crusades on behalf of the masses. His formula worked. Hearst stole some of Joseph Pulitzer's thunder in New York, then fought his way into the tough Chicago newspaper market. He had to fight so hard in Chicago that some people credit him with starting that city's tradition of gang warfare with his efforts to establish his *Chicago American* there.

His next conquest was a piece of cake. He was invited to start a newspaper in Los Angeles. To be sure, it wasn't the Los Angeles newspaper barons who invited him, nor the city's business leaders. It was the city's union activists, who realized that the union movement had an exceedingly bleak future in Los Angeles as long as Gen. Harrison Gray Otis, publisher of the *Los Angeles Times*, dominated the town. So they asked Hearst, the friend of the workingman, to start a new paper in Los Angeles that would compete with the

Times. Barely able to conceal his glee, Hearst agreed to do just that. He was so confident of success that he named the new paper after his first, the *San Francisco Examiner,* and set it up to compete head to head, in the morning, with the mighty *Los Angeles Times.* (A few years later, Hearst established the *Los Angeles Herald-Express*—or *Her-Ex*—as his afternoon standardbearer in that city.) The unions, pathetically eager to rid themselves of Otis, greeted the opening of the *Los Angeles Examiner* with fireworks, a parade, and an advance subscription list 50,000 names long. But had the dedicated unionists who paraded in gratitude to Hearst known what his descendants' attitude toward labor would be, they might have veered from their route of march, charged into the *Examiner*'s lobby, and destroyed the paper before its first edition was printed.

Hearst's life was so dramatic that only movies of such vast scope and ambition as *Citizen Kane,* which some critics consider the best movie ever made, even partly capture it. Similarly, his newspapers—with their hard-drinking, wisecracking newsmen, their glamorous sob sisters, their invisible ethics, and their all too visible screaming headlines—were so dramatic that they inspired a raft of Hollywood newspaper movies. These included not only *Front Page,* which has been remade four times, once for every generation since Hearst rode to prominence, but also a seemingly endless series of Hollywood variations on that theme. No one will ever make a movie, however, about the Hearst newspapers from Hearst's death until 1974; slow decay is not a popular Hollywood motif.

Hearst's turn to conservatism, the maturation of the American newspaper reader, and, finally, the master's death—appropriately, Hearst's body was taken to Pierce Brothers funeral home, a company on which a later media mogul, Joseph Allbritton, would partly base his fortune—vastly changed his empire. From a massive machine for the production of excitement and change it became a very rich corporation run by people who, for a long while, seemed not to like newspapers very much.

None of Hearst's five sons seemed to be empire builders. (Two of them, though, showed a real talent and interest in aviation. Perhaps flying, with its stark risk-taking, its obvious drama, and the feeling many fliers had that they were lords of the universe, exercised the same magnetic attraction on the Hearst sons that the wide-open newspaper business had exercised on their father.)

But William Randolph Hearst wanted the boys to go into the newspaper business, his newspaper business, and a man whose corporate fortune was second only to Henry Ford's wasn't going to be refused by anyone. One by one, he forced his sons to drop out of college, no matter how well they were doing—Hadn't he dropped out of college? Hadn't he done well for himself?—and take high-paying jobs with the Hearst Corporation. His last will and testament anchored them to their desks for life. According to that document, any son who left the business and struck out on his own would be reduced to an income of $30,000 a year, sheer poverty for a scion of W. R. Hearst. None of the boys exercised this option.

Hearst's dictates might have made sense had his sons been given any real power in the corporation, but Hearst bestowed that on nonfamily executives. While those executives concentrated on the company's other holdings, the substance drained out of most of the Hearst newspapers, including the *Los Angeles Herald-Express*. By the early 1950s, under publisher David Hearst, one of the Hearst sons, it had hit rock bottom. Although it still looked like the kind of newspaper that had made its founder into Citizen Hearst, one of the richest and most powerful men in America, all that remained of the old *Herald-Express* were its screaming headlines and its preoccupation with crime news. It had long ago ceased to challenge the businessmen who ran Los Angeles. No investigative reporting sullied its pages. Its morning sister, the *Examiner*, competing head to head with the *Times*, was Hearst's quality act in Los Angeles.

Meanwhile, the Hearst Corporation was concentrating on its magazine holdings, which were outperforming all expectations as the newspapers drooped. (The Hearst Corporation had acquired or developed some of the nation's most successful magazines, including *Cosmopolitan*, *Good Housekeeping*, *Harper's Bazaar*, *House Beautiful*, *Popular Mechanics*, *Science Digest*, *Sports Afield*, and *Town and Country*.) The company's newspaper policy seemed to be to ignore the papers until they began to lose money and then to sell or close them to avoid further losses. And, ominously, during the late 1950s, *Herald-Express* profits began to drop. Afternoon newspaper disease was about to strike. Hearst Corporation executives wanted to retain a foothold in the lucrative Los Angeles market, and felt that their morning-afternoon combination in that city gave them the capacity to remain there for the indefinite future. Something had to be done, though, to get the *Herald-Express* back on the fast track to profit.

In 1960 the Hearst corporate bosses appointed George Hearst Jr., whose right-wing views stood out even among the conservative Hearsts, to take his Uncle David's place as *Her-Ex* publisher. George Jr., and his right-wing attitudes and rigidities, took over the *Herald-Express* only a month after his contemporary, Otis Chandler, took over Hearst's arch-rival in Los Angeles, the *Los Angeles Times*. Chandler, although a hard worker like George Jr., was a flexible man, in tune with the new lifestyles. While George Jr. moved his paper to the right, Chandler moved his toward the center, away from the right-wing rigidity of his grandfather, Gen. Harrison Gray Otis, and his father, Norman Chandler. At the beginning of what was going to be one of America's great liberal eras, and a bad time for afternoon newspapers, this was an ill omen for the conservative afternoon *Los Angeles Herald-Express*.

Shortly after George Jr. took over as *Her-Ex* publisher, the Hearst Corporation dealt its own Los Angeles newspapers a stunning blow.

During the post–World War II era, no fewer than five daily newspapers had competed for the city's cornucopia of advertising dollars: the *Times* and the *Examiner* in the morning, and the *Mirror*, the *Herald-Express*, and the *News* in the afternoon.

The *News*, independently owned and liberal, appealed to one of the truly extinct peoples of our times: the Los Angeles straphangers who rode the red cars of the city's Pacific Electric (Streetcar) system. So powerful was the appeal of the tabloid *News*, and so many straphangers were there to appeal to, that the paper managed to put out editions around the clock and make money on every one of them. Making money on an afternoon paper appealed to Norman Chandler, Otis Chandler's father and his predecessor as *Los Angeles Times* publisher. A conservative, Norman Chandler thought the future would be much the same as the past, that blue-collar workers would continue to ride streetcars to their factory jobs and be hungry for tabloid afternoon newspapers to read. So, in 1948 he started the *Mirror*, the ultimate afternoon tabloid, to compete with the *News*.

The *Mirror* bore an eerie resemblance to the "underground" papers the children of its blue-collar readers would sneak into their parents' houses twenty years later. Like the undergrounds, its front page was printed sideways for better newsstand display. It ran personal classified ads, a risqué venture at the time and one that would be imitated with a vengeance by the undergrounds a generation later.

The *Mirror* knew its audience. It crusaded against organized crime and for improved rapid transit, two targets likely to appeal to its readers as they stood crowded together on jerking streetcars worrying about the money they owed their loan sharks. In fact, the *Mirror* was not only the tabloid to end all tabloids—its first-anniversary issue was the thickest tabloid ever produced—but the crusading paper to end all crusading papers as well. In its first ten weeks, it began five crusades: against loan sharks; against the presumption that alcoholism was a crime, not a disease; against black-market baby adoptions; for a cleaner city; and for better housing.

Innovative as it was, the *Mirror* never made money. In the early 1950s it did gain the circulation lead over the *News*, and by the end of 1954 the *News* had been sold to the *Mirror.* (The *Mirror* became the *Mirror-News* and the name *"Los Angeles Daily News"* wasn't heard again until 1982, when the suburban *San Fernando Valley News,* as part of an attempt to extend its reach out of the valley and into the city, renamed itself the *Los Angeles Daily News.*)

Then there were four, four heavy hitters left slugging it out in the mud and smog of the polluted Los Angeles basin. Chandler's *Times* battled Hearst's *Examiner* in the morning and Chandler's *Mirror-News,* which had become a full-size paper rather than a tabloid, traded blows with the *Herald-Express* in the afternoon.

The weakest warrior in any newspaper war is usually one of the papers with the double-barreled name, and in this case the weakest sister in this mélange was clearly the *Mirror-*

News. Hearst's merry marauders, many of whom were Angelenos who had grown up reading the paper they now worked for, loved pounding out sex stories and covering gory crimes in the neon slime of late afternoon journalism. But the *Mirror-News,* although an effective and intelligent crusader, didn't have its heart in its scandalmongering. By 1958 *Mirror-News* circulation had begun to shrink.

The Chandlers, its owners, far from having their hearts in the *Mirror,* were often repulsed by it. The Chandlers wanted to rise in Los Angeles society and to gain national respectability. To do so, they intended to make the *Los Angeles Times* a great and respected newspaper. Meanwhile, some of the stories they read in their own *Mirror-News* made them ill. The Chandlers also were interested in retaining the family fortune, not squandering it, and the *Mirror-News* was losing $2 million a year. If, the Chandlers thought, they could kill the *Mirror-News* and drive a stake through its heart, they would be much better off.

The only reason they kept it going was to challenge what would otherwise have been Hearst's afternoon monopoly. The Chandlers' morning *Times* led the Hearsts' morning *Examiner* strongly in both circulation and advertising, while the Chandlers' afternoon *Mirror-News* lagged slightly behind the Hearsts' afternoon *Herald-Express,* but the Chandlers feared that if they closed the *Mirror-News,* their overall advantage would melt away as fast as a Los Angeles hillside during a late winter flood, because Hearst would then be able to offer advertisers the only morning-evening combination in town.

Then Norman Chandler came up with an idea. Why not offer to close his own money-losing afternoon paper if Hearst would close his relatively high-quality, moneymaking morning paper? In April 1959 Chandler proposed just that to the

Hearst Corporation. Chandler might as well have made his proposal on the first of the month, because such an "offer" could only have been meant for April fools. Even in 1959 the bacillus of afternoon newspaper disease was firmly implanted in the raging giants of the afternoon. Los Angeles' morning papers outsold its evening papers and carried more advertising. Chandler was asking the Hearsts to give up a morning newspaper with a great future to concentrate on an afternoon newspaper with a dim future.

The Hearst execs, predictably, blew Chandler a raspberry. For two years he sulked, and all four newspapers continued the war. The only gains were made by Chandler's morning *Times,* which increased its circulation lead over Hearst's morning *Examiner,* and Hearst's afternoon *Her-Ex,* which increased its circulation lead over Chandler's afternoon *Mirror-News.* Once again, Chandler made the same offer, and this time the Hearst execs were so impressed by the *Her-Ex's* performance they decided it was the paper to bet on and accepted Chandler's choice. They agreed to fold their morning paper if Chandler folded his evening paper, the *Mirror-News.*

At the moment the Hearsts agreed to this switch, the *Mirror-News* repaid the Chandlers the $25 million they had spent on it over the previous thirteen years. It would have been a good buy at four times its cost, since it gave Chandler the bait with which he lured the half-blind Hearsts into their amazing Technicolor blunder.

Occasionally, Angelenos under thirty wonder why the giant *Los Angeles Times,* which dominates Los Angeles, and through its sister newspapers packs a heavy punch in Hartford, Dallas, Denver, and New York, is published from a building on Times Mirror Square. Norman Chandler could tell them.

"Dumb," "stupid," "ignorant," and "blind" are the high-est of compliments when applied to the Hearsts' decision, one of the worst decisions ever made by any large private firm anywhere. One former *Her-Ex* executive described it as "the worst thing that ever happened." The only corporate deci-sion that came close to rivaling it was the Ford Motor Com-pany's decision a few years before to go full speed ahead with the Edsel.

Perhaps the Hearst organization should not be faulted for failing to foresee the full extent of afternoon newspaper dis-ease. But the disease soon became epidemic in Los Angeles. While straphangers were major readers of afternoon news-papers in big cities, the public transit systems in most cities were declining. The Los Angeles public transit system never went into a serious decline, however. It wasn't allowed to live that long. One year the red cars were carrying thousands of people around town. The next year the tracks were ripped up and the cars sold. The straphangers who hadn't already bought cars now had to buy them to get to work, and, unable to read while negotiating the city's soon crowded freeways, they cut back on their afternoon newspaper purchases.

Other cities were spreading out, turning the surrounding farmland into subdivisions and shopping centers, and adding mile after mile of crowded suburban shopping streets, fes-tooned with finicky red lights. This was the gauntlet run by afternoon newspaper circulation people everywhere. But some of these cities still had public transit systems, and no city among them was booming the way Los Angeles was.

Los Angeles was expanding at incredible speed in all direc-tions, gobbling up thousands of acres of orchard and pasture every year as it surged outward. With no public transit sys-tem other than buses, a small downtown core, many major employers on its outskirts, and year-round sunshine that people wanted to enjoy in backyards, the city had no reason to build upward, so it sprawled. Soon its far-flung neighborhoods and suburbs were linked only by freeways that became impassable just when afternoon papers were sent on their way to their readers. Very soon, in fact, Los Angeles had grown into an afternoon paper's nightmare: a terribly rich city, bronzed and beautiful, sprawled naked in the sun, but impossible to reach when you needed to reach her. This was the city in which the Hearst Corporation decided to stake its all on afternoon newspaper publishing.

What made the deal even worse for Hearst was that Los Angeles was the capital of the movie and television industries, a city where, in the words of afternoon newspaper chieftain Jim Bellows, "people don't read." Even in the 1980s, the *Los Angeles Times*, indisputably one of the best newspapers in America, is read by only 25 percent of the population. This was the city in which the Hearst-Chandler deal positioned the second-rate and demoralized *Her-Ex* against the rising power of TV's evening news, which was just beginning to flex its electronic muscles.

Aside from the increasing lead the *Her-Ex* was taking over the *Mirror-News*, the only other available explanation for the massive blunder of the Hearst-Chandler deal is the rumor that Chandler paid Hearst $1.3 million to shut down the *Examiner* and move the corporation's entire Los Angeles operation to the afternoon. This rumor may have been sparked by Hearst's payment of just this amount in severance pay to the laidoff employees of the folded *Examiner*. But the millions Hearst spent and is still spending to keep the *Her-Ex* afloat dwarf that amount into insignificance, even if it actually was paid.

The Hearst organization ignored what many saw as one of the pro-Hearst aspects of the Hearst-Chandler deal. Nothing in it would have prevented the Hearst Corporation from killing the inferior *Her-Ex* and moving the superior *Examiner* to the afternoon. After all, Hearst no longer had to fear competition from the goremongers at the *Mirror-News*. They were gone. Hearst's only remaining competition was from the high-class whiz kids at the *Times*. Anyway, television news would soon preempt the market for pictures of bodies being carried away from murder scenes. The successful newspaper of the future would interpret and investigate and explore and make an increasingly complex world understandable to its increasingly frustrated readers.

Dumping the *Her-Ex*, the paper of the past, and merely moving the *Examiner*, the paper of the future, to the afternoon, would have been too smart for the Hearsts. Speculation at the time was that George Hearst Jr. didn't want to stay in the morning and fight the *Times*; he wanted to compete against no one in the afternoon, and since he had become a corporate favorite, the company let him have his way. So the Hearst Corporation closed the *Examiner* and, putting the seal of death on its remaining Los Angeles paper, changed its name, in memoriam, to the *Los Angeles Herald Examiner.* The *Times* now owned the expanding morning, and the *Her-Ex* was the unchallenged lord of the shrinking afternoon.

The *Her-Ex*, in spite of its name change (which didn't change its nickname), remained essentially the same newspaper. But the *Times* soon changed. When it was competing with three or four other papers, the Chandlers felt compelled to keep it a right-wing Republican paper to keep a lock on its right-wing Republican audience. But once it was challenged only by the old-fashioned *Her-Ex*, Otis Chandler, its new publisher, began to see its potential audience as everyone in the Los Angeles area, or at least everyone upscale, and the paper became more liberal and modern in its news coverage and its editorial views.

Paradoxically, its self-improvement program and its move to the center were aided by its right-wing antiunion past. Since it wasn't unionized, it was free to fire those people its executives thought wouldn't be able to survive the demands of a revitalized *Times*. It was also free to hire many of the excellent *Examiner* reporters who were now jobless. So it was able to prepare for the fight ahead by improving its own staff. But the tightly unionized *Her-Ex* couldn't even hire its fellow Hearst reporters from the *Examiner* because it couldn't fire any to make room for them. The *Her-Ex* editors watched mournfully while the *Examiner* reporters, in many cases superior to their own staffers, marched off to join the opposition. The Peck's bad boys at the *Her-Ex* found themselves and their inadequacies fighting single-handedly against a revitalized *Times*, reinforced with former *Examiner* reporters, now unchallenged in its secure morning bastion and eager for Hearst blood.

This did not endear the unions to *Her-Ex* publisher George Hearst Jr., who was feeling strong, because the immediate effect of the Hearst-Chandler deal was to strengthen the *Her-Ex*. Many Hearst loyalists, deprived of their Hearst paper in the morning, switched to the *Her-Ex*, the Hearst paper of the afternoon. And many former *Mirror-News* readers, deprived of their afternoon paper, also switched to the *Her-Ex*. In the immediate aftermath of the Hearst-Chandler deal, *Her-Ex* circulation grew to 720,000, bringing it within 50,000 of the *Times'* circulation. That was the closest it ever came. Its new circulation allowed it to claim the title, for a brief period, of America's largest afternoon newspaper, a title later claimed by both the *Philadelphia Bulletin* and the *Washington Star*, both dead within a few years of moving to the first rank. An Ozymandias complex may be at work here: rising to such glorious heights may blind a paper to the yawning abyss in front of it.

It certainly blinded George Hearst Jr. He was infuriated when union seniority and hiring rules prevented him from dumping the deadwood on his staff and filling their places with experienced *Examiner* reporters for the coming competition with the *Times*. He turned livid when, three years after the Hearst-Chandler deal, afternoon newspaper disease set in with a vengeance, the *Her-Ex* began losing money and subscribers, and union rules still bound him tight.

George Jr.'s grandfather, the original Hearst, had capitalized on already existing trends in American society when he built his empire. The growth in public literacy and the nationwide reaction to the exploitative practices of the nineteenth-century robber barons undergirded the Hearst chain's explosive growth. But George Jr. became a throwback to the robber barons themselves. In 1967, near the crest of one of the most liberal eras in recent American history, George Jr. decided that he was going to take a stand his grandfather had thundered against in the 1890s. He would make his paper union-free. He would drive the unions from the temple of the *Herald Examiner*.

The *Her-Ex* union leaders might have been forgiven for wondering why he was picking on them. Union work rules were vexing, true, but *Her-Ex* reporters were paid less than reporters on any other major newspaper in America. Hearst, though, was determined to rid himself of these leeches. He ignored afternoon newspaper disease, the *Her-Ex*'s mediocrity, and improvements at the *Times* as possible underlying causes for the *Her-Ex*'s shrinking circulation. The unions were responsible and they would pay.

When the *Her-Ex*'s union contracts expired in 1967, and negotiations for new contracts began, George Jr. lined up strikebreakers, moved cots, food, and portable showers into the building, and prepared to publish without a single union employee. Unaware of management's preparations, the unions proposed pathetically moderate raises for their employees. The Newspaper Guild, representing editorial employees, asked only for raises equal to those recently granted by the *Long Beach Independent Press Telegram*, a much smaller paper. George Jr. refused. As the strike deadline approached, the union leaders, perhaps sensing George Jr.'s intentions, offered to accept lower raises than those granted by the *Press Telegram* if only the *Her-Ex* would show some sign of good faith by budging from its initial offer. The response: no. At 11:00 A.M. on December 15, 1967, the unions called their members out on strike.

They never returned. To guard against sabotage, George Jr. boarded up the *Her-Ex*'s windows and strung barbed wire around the building. A stationwagon known as a "scab cab," staffed by ex-weightlifters, picked up nonstriking employees and brought them to work, changing its route every day. Cars loaded with strong-arm men followed *Her-Ex* delivery trucks to foil potential union attempts to stop them. Those *Her-Ex* employees who remained in the plant ate catered breakfasts, lunches, and dinners there and worked sixteen-hour days six days a week.

The *Her-Ex* unions spent six years on strike and doled out $6 million in strike pay to their unemployed members. Then they gave up. George Jr. had won.

But for all the good this did the *Herald Examiner* in the general community and in the business world, George Jr. might as well have run up a red flag over the building and moved to Moscow. Once the unions realized that George Jr. wasn't just maneuvering for financial advantage, but meant to be rid of them permanently, they went for his groin: his advertisers. National union leaders organized a nationwide boycott of twelve of the biggest *Her-Ex* advertisers, including the May Company, Sears Roebuck, and J. C. Penney. Local union officials went around urging local advertisers to stop advertising in the *Herald Examiner*. Some of the firms might have ignored a boycott, but striking *Her-Ex* employees or their sympathizers broke hundreds of windows in advertisers' stores and lobbed stink bombs into theaters that persisted in advertising in the *Her-Ex*. "All you needed was a marble and a slingshot" to break expensive plate-glass windows, one former *Her-Ex* editor noted. After an advertiser's windows were trashed three or four times, he was unlikely to continue his *Her-Ex* advertising. The *Her-Ex* itself, in a front-page editorial, listed 150 incidents of what it called union intimidation.

As public opinion became more and more aroused, Governor Brown and Sam Yorty, mayor of Los Angeles, tried to bring George Jr. and the unions together. But a three-man panel appointed by Yorty finally concluded that management didn't want to settle. Management wanted the unions out—permanently. As a result, public opinion, which might have sided with the *Her-Ex*, went the other way. Union members and sympathizers were already boycotting the paper. Now liberals began to do so as well. The boycott eventually became so thorough and so widespread that many people in Los Angeles today believe the strike shut down the *Herald Examiner* and that it no longer publishes.

Meanwhile, the nonunion *Los Angeles Times*, helped along by its morning monopoly, grew more and more popular as the *Her-Ex* began losing readers, an average of 35,000 a year, year after year after year. Its advertising also plummeted. By 1976 the *Her-Ex* had lost half its readers and almost two thirds of its advertising.

The *Her-Ex* had become union-free, though. It also had its remaining 350,000 readers and an afternoon monopoly in the

nation's third largest city. If George Jr. had been truly vision-
ary, he could have spent some money and made the *Her-Ex* a
great newspaper, attracting back the readers and advertisers
he had lost while the strike itself faded slowly into the mists
of the past. Instead, he pinched pennies, taking out his revenue losses on *Her-Ex* employees. After all, they had no union
to protect them now, so who was to stop him? Employee
benefits were cut. Salaries were allowed to languish as the
cost of living rose. A time clock was installed for editorial
and advertising employees. The *Her-Ex* building, and the
newspaper itself, were allowed to decay. No story was written
that might offend an advertiser. Investigative reporting was
eliminated; brief official news became the rule. As time
passed, editions and pages disappeared along with most of
the paper's best writers. *Her-Ex* news coverage, never that
good, became so spotty it was called a "guerrilla operation"
in comparison to the encyclopedic coverage of the *Los
Angeles Times*.

The paper became so thin that it advertised itself as "a
newspaper for people who don't have all day to read one."
When Patty Hearst, George Jr.'s cousin, was kidnapped, and
the people of Los Angeles turned to the *Her-Ex* to read, at the
very least, the Hearst view of the tragic event, the *Her-Ex*
responded by printing wire-service coverage of the kidnap-
ping to save the paper the cost of sending a reporter four
hundred miles north to San Francisco to cover the event.
There was little dissension in 1974 when *MORE*, the journalism review, ranked the *Her-Ex* as one of America's ten
worst newspapers. That old Hearst magic was working again.
George Jr. had pushed past approximately eighteen hundred
other American newspapers to snag the coveted honor for the
Herald Examiner. Was this what he had defeated the unions
for?

None of this sat too well with the *Her-Ex* employees. Some had been, in the words of a former *Her-Ex* editor, "picked up off the street" during the strike, but many others had been attracted to the paper by the chance to go straight from journalism school to a big-city daily. Once they got there, though, it didn't take them long to realize they had arrived long before their time at the bottom of the heap. As their salaries continued to shrink in relation to the cost of living and management continued to treat them with contempt, the *Her-Ex* employees decided that what they needed was—a union. Petitions started circulating within the Spanish-style building, the National Labor Relations Board was contacted, and by 1976 the *Her-Ex* employees were unionized once more. This time, though, one local, under the aegis of the International Printing and Graphic Communications Union, represented all employee categories at the paper, the first time in the newspaper business that all employees of a major metropolitan newspaper were represented by a single union. George Jr.'s antiunion policy had not been a total success.

The next year, *Los Angeles* magazine printed an article by Bob Gottlieb revealing that George Jr. was the president of a private concern, Southern California Contractors Incorporated, that was doing profitable business with the *Her-Ex* as that paper lay dying. Six SCCI companies, the article noted, did construction, repair, and trucking for the paper, provided it with guard service, sold it uniforms and office supplies, did its accounting, and provided it with advertising linage information (replacing the national and respected Media Records firm). This last SCCI company, Westport, Inc., *Los Angeles* magazine said, was run by two sons of George Jr. and of George Sjostrom, the *Herald*'s general manager. No one ever alleged there was anything illegal about any of this, and most

of the SCCI companies did as good a job as competing independent firms might have done, and at a lower cost. The
magazine pointed out that the Hearst Corporation had
known about SCCI all along, but the impression the SCCI
revelations conveyed was that George Jr. was sucking the
paper dry as it went down, bleeding it for his own financial
gain when he should have been spending all his efforts at
propping it up.

Soon the Hearst organization promoted George Jr. to the
position of Hearst Corporation vice president with responsibility for the overall management of the company's real
estate interests. Now the giant corporation had to figure out
what to do with the dying *Herald Examiner.*

CHAPTER EIGHT

Off the Ropes

The *Her-Ex* Tries a Comeback

Think about it a minute. If you were the Hearst Corporation, whom would you hire to replace the newly promoted George Hearst Jr.? Another Hearst? Unlikely. Perhaps Patty?

Seriously, what you would need is an establishment figure, a solid citizen, maybe a midwesterner, a Republican, of course—the Hearsts were solid Republican—but not a Goldwater type and certainly not a crook. Yes, what was needed was Frank Dale, a solid midwestern Republican, for eight years publisher of the *Cincinnati Enquirer,* and a local Republican party chieftain and fundraiser. His success at party work and as a publisher had brought him to the attention of Richard Nixon, who, knowing a good thing when he saw one, made Dale the chairman of the Committee to Re-Elect the President (CREEP).

"Hey, wait a minute," a voice chimes in. "I thought you said the Hearst Corporation wanted a guy with clean hands. The only reason anyone still remembers CREEP is that Woodward and Bernstein immortalized it during their Watergate investigation." Yes, but the fact that the scandal never came anywhere near Dale proved to the Hearst moguls that he was just the man they wanted. A guy who could associate

173

with the crooks at CREEP without getting his hands dirty could dance rings around whatever petty corruption existed at the *Herald Examiner.*

Dale, along with a number of other Nixon backers, had been given a position that carried ambassadorial rank, U.S. envoy to the United Nations organizations in Geneva, Switzerland. Then when Jimmy Carter was elected, Nixon's supporters guessed their services as the president's personal representatives would no longer be required. Dale was swiftly appointed publisher of the *Los Angeles Herald Examiner.* (Dale's hiring was part of the Hearst Corporation's revitalization of its ailing newspaper division.)

His first gestures were symbolic, but they were just the sort of gestures the *Her-Ex* needed. He removed the time clocks that the demoralized reporters and ad salesmen had been required to punch, and repaired the huge digital clock on the front of the *Her-Ex* building to let the people know that even the Hearst Corporation knew what time it was. And he replaced the scowling security guard in the lobby with a smiling secretary.

All this was good image building, and good for staff morale, but what the paper needed was a new staff, at least at the top. The paper's circulation and advertising, shrinking under George Jr., was still shrinking, and Dale couldn't stop it on his own. He was a publisher, a money raiser, an organizer, and a diplomat, not an editor.

There was an editor newly available who had a wealth of experience in getting afternoon papers noticed and talked about—Jim Bellows, who had just quit his job as editor of the *Washington Star* under Joe Allbritton. Bellows was immediately hired as editor of the *Herald Examiner.*

While Dale played the good guy, Bellows occasionally played the heavy, and he did so on this occasion, firing thirty reporters and editors within six months. They included almost the entire staff of the entertainment section, which Bellows, very aware of the fact that he was now in Los Angeles, saw as the paper's core gone rotten. Bellows ended the old *Her-Ex* practice of allowing entertainment companies and sports teams to provide free tickets for, and pay the traveling expenses of, *Her-Ex* reporters.

Bellows surprised very few with the other editorial changes he soon put in place at the *Her-Ex*. He had run a "Question and Answer" feature down the lefthand side of the *Washington Star*'s front page, so he ran a "Question and Answer" feature down the lefthand side of the *Los Angeles Herald Examiner*'s front page. (Its first subject: Bob Dylan.) He had run an "In Focus" analysis feature across the bottom of the *Washington Star*'s front page, so he ran a "Bottom Line" analysis feature across the bottom of the *Her-Ex*'s front page. (Its name later was changed to "News Focus.") He had instituted a Writer-in-Residence program at the *Star*, so he started one at the *Her-Ex*. He had run an irreverent, saucy gossip column called "Ear" in the *Star*, so he ran an irreverent, saucy gossip column called "Page 2" in the *Her-Ex*, dealing mostly with local media people and entertainers.

"Ear" had picked on *Washington Post* executive editor Ben Bradlee and his roommate then, *Post* writer Sally Quinn, calling them the "Fun Couple" and the staid *Post* the "Other Paper," or "O.P." Although the top editors at the *Los Angeles Times* protected themselves from "Page 2" by holding their marriages together, the *Times* was quickly dubbed the "Usepaper," or "U.P.," by the gang at "Page 2" (the *Times* having called itself the "Usepaper" in its own advertisements).

Bellows wasn't just inanely repeating himself. The situation he was facing in Los Angeles resembled the situation he had been facing in Washington. In each city the dominant newspaper took itself too seriously and left itself open to deft pricking. And in each city, Bellows thought, there were thousands of newspaper readers who yearned for a lighter touch.

Washington, though, was the nation's political capital, whereas Los Angeles was its entertainment capital, so Bellows knew he could go a little further in Los Angeles. If Los Angeles readers weren't interested in the flip, the zingy, the jazzed-up, and the side-splittingly funny, then who would be? And who was more willing to provide them with such copy than Bellows, who loved writers and barely tolerated reporters?

When Bubbles, the two-ton hippo at the local Lion Country Safari, decided she had been gawked at long enough and heavy-footed it into the Los Angeles hills, eventually making her new home in the middle of a lake, Bellows was beside himself with joy and anticipation. Now he would show those deadheads at the "Usepaper" how to cover a living, breathing human-interest story. Now he'd throw his own kind of mud.

After covering the escape itself, the *Her-Ex* began a new daily feature on page 1 called "Hippo Watch," with its own editor, the "Hippo Editor," who speculated on Bubbles' whereabouts and solicited reader suggestions about the great hippo hunt, Bubbles' inner life, the morality of hippo hunting, and other heavy issues. "Hippo Watch" ran for three solid weeks, attracting eleven thousand letters from readers, and crowding most news off the front page. Only a short while after arriving in Los Angeles, Bellows was in hippo heaven.

Bellows also went after entertainment in a different sense altogether. He reasoned that since entertainment was a big industry in Los Angeles, one should try to entertain, but one should also try to cover entertainment.

In demolishing the former *Her-Ex* entertainment staff, Bellows had ruled out, or at least played down, puffery: cheesecake photos of new starlets, articles written by press agents about new movies under production, and speculative stories about the lives of the stars. Los Angelenos were used to that. They could buy that sort of junk at the supermarket along with their day-old bread. But Bellows thought they might be, hoped they would be, interested in what was going on behind the entertainment scenes.

News stories about David Begelman in national newspapers had stirred up a lot of interest, showing that Americans were interested in minute details of personality and betrayal, even within corporate structures, especially if the story had something to do with entertainment. (Begelman had resigned as a director and executive vice president of Columbia Pictures after being accused of obtaining $61,000 in corporate funds for his personal use.) The *Los Angeles Times* didn't spend much energy on entertainment coverage of this sort. The Begelman story had been heavily covered by the out-of-town newspapers long before the ponderous *Times* got around to mentioning it in its long gray columns.

So Bellows recruited his former assistant managing editor at the *Star*, Mary Anne Dolan, and put her in charge of *Her-Ex* entertainment coverage. Dolan immediately spotted a chink in the local Goliath's armor. The lordly *Los Angeles Times*, thinking it had nothing to fear from the *Her-Ex*, often waited awhile before bothering to review a theatrical or musical event, leaving its poor readers—where else could they go?— either to waste the price of a ticket to a worthless show or to miss a good production. Dolan started running *Her-Ex* reviews the day after the opening of each event. To assure her reviewers they had absolute freedom, she even revoked the long-standing Hearst injunction against praising the movie

Citizen Kane. (The main character in the movie—Charles Foster Kane—was transparently William Randolph Hearst.)

Dale, Bellows, and Dolan also gave new impetus to the *Herald Examiner*'s investigative reporting.

Under Dolan's supervision, reporter Merle Linda Wolin produced a long series called "Sweatshop." To get the story, Wolin posed as a Brazilian immigrant and worked in several Los Angeles sweatshops, then traced the garments she helped make to wholesalers and boutiques. Partly because undercover reporting had been criticized by various journalistic authorities, including the Pulitzer Prize board, Wolin, after finishing her undercover work, went back to everyone she had talked to, identified herself as a reporter, and reinterviewed them. Dolan shrewdly exploited Wolin's work. Many of the workers in the sweatshops were Hispanic, so Dolan arranged to have the articles translated and reprinted in a Spanish-language newspaper and persuaded a Spanish-language radio station to read the articles over the air each day.

The Dolan-Wolin team almost made it to the top; the sweatshop series came very close to winning a Pulitzer. Because the Pulitzer board disapproved of undercover reporting, however, it ignored its own public service jury's unanimous recommendation that the series be awarded a Pulitzer, and granted the prize instead to an entry it had transferred from another category. One would think the board might have learned something from the year before, when it also transferred entries around and ended up awarding a Pulitzer to the phony *Washington Post* story about a nonexistent eight-year-old heroin addict.

If the *Her-Ex* staff was upset by its close brush with Pulitzer fame, soon thereafter the sweatshop series received what was, for a Los Angeles newspaper with a focus on the entertainment industry, an even greater accolade: Francis Ford Coppola bought the series with the intention of making a two-hour TV movie out of it. Coppola announced that after the movie ran on NBC, it would be dubbed in Spanish for showing on Spanish-language TV stations.

In any case, other prize juries treated the *Her-Ex* with more consideration. In 1979 and 1980, and again in 1983, the *Her-Ex*, formerly the laughingstock of the journalistic world, won more first-place awards for journalistic excellence in the Greater Los Angeles Press Club competition than did the *Los Angeles Times*, one of the journalism world's greatest totems.

The new *Her-Ex* team also changed the paper's editorial-page stance from right wing to middle of the road, improved its sports coverage, and worked to improve its local coverage. In Washington, Bellows had tried to put more local news into the *Star* than there was in the *Post*. There was no way he could do that in Los Angeles—on some days a *Her-Ex* could be hidden inside a *Times* and not even be noticed—but he could find local stories the *Times* had missed and give them prominent display.

One such story was the killing of a black woman, Eula Love, by two Los Angeles police officers following an argument over an unpaid $89 utility bill. The *Times* ran one paragraph on the story—on page 2.

Bellows and company thought the story deserved better. Love had carried an eleven-inch boning knife, but the two officers were armed with police revolvers and had shot her eight times. The *Her-Ex* played the story big on its front page from the very beginning, making the case a cause célèbre and inspiring an official Los Angeles police investigation. The *Los Angeles Times* didn't move the story to page 1 until three months after the shooting.

All these innovations were aimed at adding Los Angeles' upscales, especially the women and the young professionals among them, to the *Her-Ex*'s traditional readers: aging, male blue-collar workers who were unattractive to advertisers. Bellows, Dale, and Dolan attracted some of these readers, and certainly got the paper talked about, but getting talked about mattered much less in Los Angeles than in Washington.

Bellows has always argued that there are only three industries in D.C.: law, the bureaucracy, and the media. If by attacking Washington's "Other Paper" you get the media community talking about the *Star*, the two other industries, and thus the entire city, soon hear about the paper.

In diverse, sprawling Los Angeles, however, you throw a newspaper into the forest and nobody hears it fall. It's talked about in the media community, a relatively small one, and that's that. And the *Times*, in comparison with the *Her-Ex*, had much more circulation and cash than had the *Washington Post* vis-à-vis the *Star*. (The *Times* also had four reporters for every *Her-Ex* reporter; more people worked in the *Los Angeles Times* newsroom than in the entire *Her-Ex* building.) To make things worse, because of the relatively low pay at the *Her-Ex*, that paper's reporters were constantly leaving after only a year or two for better-paying jobs.

The editors at the *Times* also used their cash, and their own savvy, to imitate many *Herald Examiner* innovations. *Times* writing became more human and more colorful. The paper jumped on local stories faster and played them better, and its entertainment coverage improved; the *Herald Examiner* had wakened the *Times* to its shortcomings. All of this was a great service for the newspaper-reading public, but some at the *Her-Ex* found it discouraging, and in any case the *Her-Ex*'s circulation and its advertising share continued to decline.

Bellows, who felt that the Hearst Corporation wasn't spending enough money promoting the newspaper, left in 1981 to become editor of "Entertainment Tonight," a television show.

But Dale and the Hearst Corporation, instead of retreating, decided to take a great leap forward. They appointed Mary Anne Dolan editor of the *Her-Ex* in Bellows' place. Dolan was perfectly well qualified for the job. She had been assistant managing editor of the *Washington Star* and assistant managing editor and then managing editor of the *Her-Ex*. The only thing unusual about her as *Her-Ex* editor was her gender. Despite hundreds of years of female participation in the news business, it wasn't until a major newspaper was as far behind as the *Her-Ex*—its circulation had fallen to 284,000, compared with the *Los Angeles Times'* one million—that it found the courage to appoint a woman to its top spot. Dolan, in 1981, became the first female to be appointed editor of a major metropolitan newspaper in the United States.

Meanwhile, Dale and the Hearst Corporation were working on two plans to turn the paper's fortunes around. Hearst had finally remembered that it was the nation's largest privately held company and began to act the part. Suburban papers were luring away advertisers? Buy the suburban papers! Readers and advertisers were deserting the *Her-Ex* because it came out in the afternoon? Move it to the morning!

In mid-1981 the company spent $15–$20 million to purchase twenty-eight weeklies and two dailies, all within Los Angeles County but in areas where the *Her-Ex* itself was weak. It was hardly a coincidence that on one day a week, when all of Hearst's dailies and weeklies published simultaneously, the combined circulation of the *Herald* and its newly acquired satellites hit the 700,000 notch the *Herald* had occupied before it began its long slide, and that the new purchases gave the *Her-Ex* and its new acquisitions the circulation lead over the *Times* in Los Angeles County on that day.

By staying within the county, the *Her-Ex* was contrasting itself sharply with the *Times'* tendency to go rollicking off on what amounted to foreign adventures. The Times Mirror Company had purchased *Newsday*, in New York, a paper just about as far away from Los Angeles as you can get and still be in the U.S., as well as the *Dallas Times-Herald* and the *Denver Post*. The *Times* itself had expanded locally in pursuit of upscale readers by opening an Orange County edition in 1968 and a San Diego edition in 1978. In 1974 the paper had canceled its Central Zone edition, which served downtown Los Angeles, clearly indicating its priorities.

Readers of the far-flung *Los Angeles Times* regional editions may eventually abandon those editions in favor of more local papers, but the readers of the newly acquired *Herald*-owned papers will already be reading their local papers. And by purchasing already publishing suburban and community newspapers, the *Her-Ex* avoided the immense detail involved in publishing its own regional or suburban editions, detail that already had helped suffocate the *Washington Star* and certainly wasn't helping the *Los Angeles Times*.

The suburban and community newspaper purchases, bold as they were, may not have been bold enough, however. In a metropolitan area as vast as Los Angeles, Hearst's thirty newly purchased newspapers were barely noticeable in the dust and smoke generated by three hundred weeklies and twenty-two dailies fighting for predominance in Los Angeles and Orange counties alone. They also left gaps in advertising coverage for other papers, especially the *Times*, to exploit.

Some of those gaps were in the very areas, such as West Los Angeles, where the *Her-Ex* most wanted to attract young upscale readers. And soon after Hearst bought the papers, their advertising linage dropped when, following an industrywide trend, advertisers began sending some ads through the mail rather than including them as inserts in newspapers.

The Hearst Corporation soon tried another move, unprecedented for a paper as big as the *Her-Ex* still was: moving the paper to the morning. (Many smaller papers have made this switch in one day, but the *Her-Ex* was saddled with independent delivery contractors it had to replace one by one to make the switch work, so the move took eighteen months.) Moving to the morning allowed the *Her-Ex* to challenge the *Los Angeles Times* on its own time turf for the readers the *Times* might be missing: those who disliked its bulk, its gray gravity, its dominance, and its tilt toward suburbia, and who wanted to read a lighter, feistier paper with its eyes on Los Angeles and not overseas.

The move to the morning, however, made more obvious another long-standing *Her-Ex* problem—its low circulation. (Some say every *Her-Ex* department except its newsroom has problems, because the paper can't attract competent executives to them; few such executives are willing to risk their careers for a paper in the grips of such life-threatening circumstances.) As circulation of the *Her-Ex* has shrunk, and as *Her-Ex* homes have become fewer and farther between, the paper's circulation problems have worsened. In some areas, only one in a hundred homes subscribes to the *Her-Ex*, making delivery of the paper in those areas expensive and inefficient.

Until recently, the *Her-Ex* didn't even know who its subscribers were. Earlier, independent dealers, partly subsidized by the *Her-Ex*, had delivered the papers. A *Her-Ex* attempt to replace the independent dealers with its own employees first ran into opposition from the state government, which was protective of the rights of independent franchisers. Then, after the *Her-Ex* had overcome this opposition in the courts, and after the transition to an employee-delivered paper was almost complete, the *Her-Ex* found out, through its newly acquired knowledge of its delivery operation, that it had even fewer subscribers than it thought it had. Some of its subscribers, Dale said, had been created out of whole cloth by dealers anxious for larger *Her-Ex* delivery subsidies (a charge the dealers deny).

Problems such as this one didn't prevent the paper from trying another extremely daring stratagem. Under editor Dolan's direction, the *Her-Ex* began emphasizing news of interest to women, moving such stories from the inside sections, where they had languished, and continue to languish in other newspapers, to the front page.

In recent issues, stories about discrimination against women by pension plans, and about a Louisiana woman who had one black great-great-great-great-grandmother and was trying to prove herself white under Louisiana law, have appeared on the front page of the *Los Angeles Herald Examiner.* Dolan also appointed a woman to write one of the paper's sports columns and another to write a column about women and religion.

The *Her-Ex*'s new emphasis certainly aided the paper in its attempt to appeal to Los Angeles–area female readers, many of whom, surveys showed, didn't read the *Times.* But the *Herald* can't play this card daily without descending into artificiality, since men are still the major players in the world of news. If the *Her-Ex* began running stories such as "Mrs. Mondale Pleased with Illinois Win" on its front page, it would soon be laughed out of the general-circulation market and forced to compete with *Ms.* and the *Ladies Home Journal.*

For six weeks in the fall of 1983, though, the *Her-Ex,* pondering yet another bold move, put out a prototype of a new Sunday newspaper to replace its existing Sunday edition. Twenty temporary editorial employees were hired to write and edit the prototype, a flashy, experimental newspaper obviously influenced by *USA Today.* The prototype boasted magazine styling, full-color photos, and a full-color weather map that showed surfing conditions as well as weather. Some ten thousand copies of each issue were printed and distributed to selected readers.

This new Sunday paper might have done well if put into regular production; according to Dale, three different independent research firms the *Her-Ex* hired said readers of the new edition loved it. But printing the new paper for more than six weeks would have required a $7 million investment in a new press, Dale said, and to recommend that such an investment be made, he decided he would have to secure year-long advertising contracts in advance. When advertisers could not be convinced to sign such contracts, Dale said, the plan had to be dropped.

For a while, the *Her-Ex* also considered giving Los Angeles the Murdoch rush, a very brightly colored, very dramatic *Her-Ex* aimed at a mass audience. The *Her-Ex*'s editors finally decided, though, that by taking the Murdoch road, they would also fall heir to Murdoch's problem: too many readers and not enough advertisers. As it is now, the *Her-Ex* needs both readers and advertisers unless it wants to spend millions printing flashy newspapers that lose money with every copy sold.

Despite the numerous setbacks the *Her-Ex* has suffered,

Dale says he remains optimistic about the paper's problems. "We're still here, and those who said when I came here that we couldn't survive have gone themselves," Dale said recently. He insists that the Hearst Corporation still wants a voice in the Los Angeles market and is willing to keep the *Her-Ex* going until that voice is secured.

If Dale wasn't optimistic, he would be suicidal. With something like nine times the *Her-Ex's* advertising, and six times its circulation, the *Los Angeles Times* looks unbeatable.

And with the *Times* so far ahead of the *Her-Ex*, it is highly unlikely that it would ever even consider a joint operating agreement with the smaller paper. The *Her-Ex* might propose a JOA with a suburban paper—the move would be unprecedented, but so was everything else the *Her-Ex* has done—but what suburban paper would want the *Her-Ex's* problems?

Dale insists, though, that the Hearst Corporation can and will continue to publish a competing daily newspaper in Los Angeles.

CHAPTER NINE

Death in the Afternoon

Despite all the newspapers it has killed, all the journalists it has put out of work, and all the readers it has left without the newspapers they preferred, afternoon newspaper disease has been of some service. It has shown which among this nation's newspaper owners possess the determination and resources to fight against lopsided odds with guts, energy, and innovation.

The disease also has demonstrated what steps won't work as antidotes:

—Starting a new afternoon newspaper.

—Letting the morning paper take the circulation lead and hoping to regain it.

—Devoting an afternoon paper to sensationalized crime and violence.

—Transforming an afternoon paper into a feature-oriented supplement to a morning paper.

Fortunately, the struggle against the disease has also shown some ways in which big-city afternoon newspapers can stave off or defeat the illness:

—Improving the threatened newspaper's news coverage early and making it as nationally and internationally oriented, on the same scale, as the morning paper, to attract the upscale readers advertisers want to reach and to offer a real contrast to the suburban papers.

—Starting a Sunday edition early and keeping it competitive.

—Moving the paper's home-delivery edition to the morning.

—Starting a morning edition while still publishing an afternoon edition (although the afternoon edition may later be closed), as a way of moving the paper's afternoon readers to the morning in gentle stages.

Fighting the disease successfully takes money, of course, and that's where advertisers will have to help, not only in the public's interest but in their own. By moving the bulk of their newspaper advertising to the top paper in each market as soon as it assumes that status, the nation's advertisers are blithely killing off the competing (i.e., afternoon) newspapers in America's big cities.

Furthermore, they are putting themselves in the grip of a small group of unregulated monopolies: the remaining (i.e., morning) papers, which, with no competition, will be infinitely freer to raise their rates than they were when competition existed. Not all advertising can be transferred to radio, TV, shoppers, magazines, or direct mail when morning newspaper advertising rates grow too steep, and advertisers who must continue to place ads in big-city morning newspapers will eventually pay the penalty for aiding and abetting death in the afternoon.

The owners of those big-city afternoon newspapers, or former afternoon newspapers, that still survive—including the *Oakland Tribune* and the *Los Angeles Herald Examiner*—not only have staved off afternoon newspaper disease, but also have been exceptionally bold and original in their choice of editors and in their approach to news and feature coverage.

As for those newspapers that failed, not all the blame for their failure need fall on afternoon newspaper disease itself. Some must fall on owners who failed to see the onslaught before it was too late. Some must fall on owners who took only timid or retrograde steps to defend themselves against the disease. And some must fall on owners who deserted their posts too hurriedly.

Owning a newspaper is not like owning a dogfood company, and shutting down a newspaper as soon as it stops spewing out profits is not a responsible action. (Newspaper owners seem to abandon their businesses more quickly than owners of other businesses, who are willing to take years of losses in order to work toward future profitability.) No one expects a for-profit company to keep a newspaper going as a charity; but such a company should take into account the years of profit it took out of its newspaper when claiming there's nothing more it can do for its suffering offspring.

Nor should all the blame fall on the owners or managers of the ailing newspapers involved. Owners of healthy newspapers who refused to lower their profit margins to keep another newspaper going within a joint operating agreement must accept a large share.

What it often comes down to is the lack of agreement about what the newspaper business really is.

In a recent movie about football, a huge football player grabbed his relatively small coach in the locker room and began shaking him, screaming, "When I say it's a game, you say it's a business! When I say it's a business, you say it's a game!" He was talking about football, of course, but analogies come to mind. When publishers want the government, or the public, to keep hands off their newspapers, they solemnly point out that newspapering is a sacred trust guaranteed to all Americans, especially newspaper owners, by the

Founding Fathers. When they want to close a newspaper, even though it has hundreds of thousands of readers, they argue that a newspaper is a business, and that if a business doesn't make money for a year or two, it must die. I'm not big enough to pick up and shake the newspaper owners of America, but if I could, I would, asking them again and again, "Is it a business or is it a sacred trust?"

Despite the survival of a number of big-city afternoon newspapers, some say that most if not all such papers are doomed. Those who shrug off the death of many of this country's major newspapers would be wise to remember what business they're talking about. Fatalism is not a healthy attitude for a major industry. To what part of the industry will such fatalism be applied next? Big-city newspapers in general? Newspapers with stories that run longer than three or four paragraphs? Newspapers not drenched with four-color maps and graphics? Newspapers in general? News gathering itself?

That fatalism has allowed, or at least encouraged, the establishment of a new system of media monopolies in most of the big cities in which afternoon newspapers have died. Only a few years ago, many of those cities had at least one morning and one evening newspaper providing different perspectives on the same events for readers not inclined to trust blindly the infallible wisdom of one newspaper and its owner.

Now, in those cities, only one newspaper covers the city and only one newspaper, at best, covers each of the suburbs. Each big-city morning newspaper covers foreign, national, and metropolitan news for all of the area's readers, and each suburban paper covers mostly suburban news for its readers. The reader rarely has access to a second version of the same story. TV and radio stations, when they're able to cover stories that don't lend themselves to visuals, take many of their ideas for such stories from the pages of the morning big-city newspaper. Specialized publications speak to their own narrow audiences, and weekly, community, and neighborhood newspapers reach relatively few readers. Computer delivery of news is just another means for the only surviving major newspaper in each area—the morning newspaper—to deliver its version of the news to readers. In the cozy monopoly niche, no competing voices ever intrude.

American journalism has a proud past. Is this the future that we, and our millions of readers, deserve?

Sources

CHAPTERS ONE AND TWO

Sources: Josephine Albright, Alice Arlen, Charles Bennett, Edward Egan, Peter Freiberg, Tom Goldstein, Andrew Hayes, Robert Hunt, Theodore Kheel, George McDonald, John Morton, Michael O'Neill, John Polich, John Reidy, Dorothy Schiff, Scott Smith, Gregory Thornton, Bruce Thorp, Arthur Wible.

Periodicals: America, Business Week, Chicago Tribune, Columbia Journalism Review, Editor & Publisher, Esquire, Forbes, Fortune, London Sunday Times, MORE, Nation, National Review, New Republic, Newsweek, New Yorker, New York News, New York Post, New York Times, Present Tense, Press, Quote-Unquote, Time, Wall Street Journal, Washington Journalism Review, Washington Post.

Books: Jeffrey Potter, *Men, Money, and Magic: The Story of Dorothy Schiff* (New York: Coward, McCann & Geoghegan, 1976).

CHAPTER THREE

Sources: Craig Ammerman, Walter Annenberg, Harry Coles Jr., Karl Eller, William Gullifer, N. S. Hayden, Diane

Lyles, Sam McKeel, William McLean III, John Malone, Edward Mumford, George Packard, Gilles Roy, J. P. Smith, Robert L. Taylor, Ray Van Landingham.

Periodicals: Center City Welcomat, Chicago Tribune, Columbia Journalism Review, Editor & Publisher, Forbes, Los Angeles Times, Newsweek, New York Times, Philadelphia Bulletin, Philadelphia Daily News, Philadelphia Inquirer, Philadelphia Magazine, Press, Quote-Unquote, Time, Wall Street Journal, Washington Journalism Review, Washington Post.

Books: John Cooney, *The Annenbergs* (New York: Simon & Schuster, 1982).

CHAPTERS FOUR AND FIVE

Sources: Charles Bear, James Bellows, William Boarman, Ray Dick, Gregg Easterbrook, Sidney Epstein, Murray Gart, Donald Graham, Fred Hiatt, Dennis Horgan, George Hoyt, Lloyd Hyson, Phillip Kadis, Llewellyn King, Howard Kurtz, Robert Linowes, Diana McLellan, John McMeel, John Malone, William Mayer, John Morton, Alison Muscatine, Crosby Noyes, Lois Romano, James Shepley, John Tarpey, Judy Weinraub.

Periodicals: Business Week, Dun's Review, Columbia Journalism Review, Editor & Publisher, Los Angeles Herald Examiner, Los Angeles Times, New Republic, Newsweek, New Yorker, New York Times, Oakland Tribune, Philadelphia Bulletin, Press, Quill, Time, U.S. News & World Report, Wall Street Journal, Washingtonian, Washington Journalism Review, Washington Monthly, Washington Post, Washington Star.

CHAPTER SIX

Sources: William Eaton, Karl Eller, Joseph W. Knowland,

Diane Lyles, Douglas McCorkindale, Francis Martin, Robert Maynard, Richard Meister, Ron Miller, Gayle Montgomery, William Mungo, Richard Paoli, John Polich, Raul Ramirez. *Periodicals:* Adweek, Columbia Journalism Review, Editor & Publisher, Honolulu Star Bulletin, Los Angeles Times, Newsweek, New York Times, Oakland Tribune, Quill, San Francisco Focus, Scene, Time, Washington Journalism Review, Washington Post.

CHAPTERS SEVEN AND EIGHT

Sources: James Bellows, Gene Bradford, Frank Dale, Robert Epstein, Patricia Lawson, John Malone, Scot Paltrow, William Ryan, Scott Schmidt, David Shaw, Stella Zadeh.

Periodicals: Columbia Journalism Review, Editor & Publisher, Esquire, Los Angeles Herald Examiner, Los Angeles Magazine, Los Angeles Times, Nation, New Republic, Newsweek, New Times, New West, New York Times, Reporter, Time, Wall Street Journal, Washington Journalism Review, Washington Post.

Books: Lindsay Chaney and Michael Cieply, *The Hearsts* (New York: Simon & Schuster, 1981); Robert Gottlieb and Irene Wolt, *Thinking Big* (New York: G. P. Putnam's Sons, 1977); Jack R. Hart, *The Information Empire* (Lanham, Md.: University Press of America, 1981); Frances G. Locher, ed., *Contemporary Authors*, vol. 102 (Detroit: Gale Research, 1981); W. A. Swanberg, *Citizen Hearst* (New York: Charles Scribner's Sons, 1961).

INDEX

Index

201